Spirit-Filled Leadership:

Portraits of the Presidents, Secretaries and Treasurers of the General Conference of Seventh-day Adventists

DeWitt S. Williams

xulon
PRESS

Spirit-Filled Leadership
Portraits of the Presidents, Secretaries and Treasurers of the General Conference of Seventh-day Adventists
by DeWitt S. Williams

Printed in the United States of America

ISBN 9781498446785

Unless otherwise indicated, scripture quotations taken from the King James Version (KJV) – public domain.

www.xulonpress.com

PREFACE

—⁓—

I t's a superb feeling to complete a project. This project took about eighteen months to finish. I have dug deeply into many old and historical sources and pulled out many interesting and intriguing facts. I would like to take a few minutes to thank those who helped me get to the finish line. First of all, I must thank the General Conference Archives. Benjamin Baker, Peter Chiomenti and David Trim answered my questions to the best of their abilities and then steered me to places that would give me the rest of my answers. I thank them for the Online Archives and for their wonderful pictures. Most of the pictures that I used came from this source.

Then, I would like to thank Andrews University Center for Adventist Research (CAR), Oakwood University Archives (Heather James, head archivist) and Loma Linda University Heritage Center and Gilbert Abella of Nelson Memorial Library, Pacific Union College. Washington Adventist University Weiss Library was also helpful in sharing from their Heritage Room. Alvin Singleton was a great help for pulling out information from online sources about dates of birth and death, parents and siblings, and difficult-to-find family information.

I would like to thank the living officers. I interviewed them over the telephone and followed up with email conversations: Ted N.C. Wilson, Jan Paulsen, Robert Folkenberg, G. Ralph Thompson, Don Gilbert, Clyde Franz, and Robert Rawson. Many times I also interviewed their secretaries and administrative assistants. Many thanks to Glenn Phillips who gave me additional information on his fellow Barbadian countryman, G. Ralph Thompson. Family members Roy Branson and Bert Beach filled in many details that obituaries left out about their family.

Special thanks go to Brian Strayer, professor of history at Andrews University. He is an expert on John Byington, John Loughborough and several of the pioneers. My greatest thanks go to him for reading the entire manuscript with a shrewd eye and pointing out any and all mistakes and making recommendations for improvements. Special thanks also go to The Ellen G. White Estate for the wonderful photos that they shared and for the input of Jim Nix and Tim Poirier.

My wife, Margaret, always encourages me and inspires me to do my best even though she is bed-ridden with muscular dystrophy. We are in our 53rd year of marriage and I don't accept appointments any more that take me away from her. So I am free to pursue my interest in Adventist history, as I am able. My daughter, Darnella, lives with me to help me care for my wife and she has a flair for words and on many occasions shared with me her youthful input and ideas.

We hope you enjoy reading about these great Adventist leaders whom I believe were inspired by God to lead the Adventist Church during a special period of their lives. For those of you interested in Neal and Ted N. C. Wilson in more detail, please see my book, *Highly Committed, The Captivating Story of the*

Wilson Family and Their Impact on the Adventist Church. This book was published in 2013 and can be ordered from Amazon or from TeachServices.com.

When I had finished the presidents I wanted to know a little more about the other two executives - the second highest officer in the church, the secretary, and the treasurer, the third officer. There was precious little about these individuals, many times not even an obituary. The brethren seemed to delight in calling each other by just two initials (E. B., A. R., and W. H., etc.) and then the last name. It was, in some instances, a challenge just to discover their full first and middle names.

I used the 2013 Annual Statistical Report for the dates of the sessions of the General Conference of Seventh-day Adventists.

May we all pledge ourselves to greater loyalty and commitment to God and the Adventist Church as we read these profiles.

Picture credits are listed under each photo or in the back of the book on pages 293 and 295.

INTRODUCTION

—⚬—

Adventist Church governance is different from national politics. With Adventist elections, there are no surveys; no Gallup or Quinnipiac polls can be taken to see who the favorite son is. With Adventist world leadership, no candidate can declare himself the most qualified in the organization and start campaigning for the presidency. Voicing such a boastful conviction, even if true, would immediately disqualify that person.

There are no organized Adventist groups like the Democratic, Republican or Independent parties that promote their candidates. It would be inappropriate for the *Adventist Review,* the official voice of the Seventh-day Adventist Church, to speculate or make predictions.

In American politics, the candidate with the most money and the greatest following has an advantage in the power struggle. Money can acquaint people through the media with a candidate's platform, abilities and vision. Debates go on ad infinitum until one candidate in each party prevails and is ready to do battle with the candidate of the other party and the debating process begins all over again. This can't happen in the Adventist Church.

The Adventist election system is quiet, calm, and very spiritual; it is usually finished in a few hours. There is no power struggle for the presidency of the world church. Leaders who have proven themselves by serving as chief officer of a division or a vice president at the General Conference are usually considered first. Because of the international nature of the Adventist Church it is rare for a pastor of a local church, no matter how effective his leadership has been, to rise to this level of leadership directly. Slowly, a leader must gain experience and prove himself spiritually and administratively, by serving in different posts.

All thirteen Divisions of Adventism make arrangements to send delegates to the church's largest meeting, convened now every five years, to select the person who will lead the flock for the ensuing quinquennium. Representation based on membership allows delegates from every nation where there is a church to gather together for their input.

This representative community of believers, with much prayer, selects a nominating committee who propose candidates. When a single name has been discussed, prayed over, and decided upon, the name is brought to the entire body of delegates for final approval. Usually the nominating begins on Friday morning and before the Sabbath begins that Friday evening, the selection has been made. The new president will present the sermon on the second Sabbath of the session.

As I have studied in great detail these officers who have led God's people for more than 150 years I am struck by their spirit of sacrifice, their devotion to the Three Angels' Messages and their desire to see the work finished so Christ can return. They were not motivated by human gain or a desire for importance. Every once in a while when the presidents who were alive during her lifetime might be tempted to feel exalted by the spirit of pride that instinctively resides in human nature, Mrs. E. G. White would orally or in writing rebuke them for the temptation to use "kingly power" or the wrong use of authority.

Dudley M. Canright felt that he should be president of the Adventist Church. Canright was a great evangelist and eloquent preacher but his desire for the presidency was motivated by his desire to be great and popular. Drury W. Reavis, a young man just out of Battle Creek College, called to work in the Ohio Conference where Canright was the president, talks about Canright's obsession with popularity and greatness. In his book, *I Remember*, D. W. Reavis tells of a conversation he had with Dudley M. Canright.

Canright and Reavis went to Chicago to study elocution at Hamill's school in 1880. They were each supposed to critique each other for the class. Reavis writes: "On Sunday night, in the largest church of the West Side, he (Canright) spoke on 'The Saints' Inheritance' to more than 3000 people and I took a seat in the gallery directly in front of him, to see every gesture and to hear every tone. . .but that was as far as I got . . .for he so quickly and eloquently launched into this, his favorite theme, that I, with the entire congregation, became entirely absorbed in the Biblical facts he was so convincingly presenting. . .

"On all sides I could hear people saying it was the most wonderful sermon they had ever heard. I knew it was not the oratorical manner of the delivery, but the Bible truth clearly and feelingly presented, that had appealed to the people-. . . I saw that the power was all in the truth, not in the speaker."

When the two of them were alone in a city park Reavis prepared to give his criticism but confessed to Canright that he had become so completely carried away with the soul-inspiring Biblical subject that he did not think once of the oratorical rules.

Suddenly Canright sprang to his feet and said "D.W. (Reavis), I believe I could become a great man were it not for our unpopular message."

Reavis stepped in front of Canright and said "D.M. (Canright), the message made you all you are, and the day you leave it, you will retrace your steps back to where it found you." Canright did leave the message and joined the Baptist Church. He became the foremost critic of Adventism and Mrs. White. But his position in the new denomination declined more and more.

James White turned down the first request of the church to place the mantle of leadership on his shoulders. White was not seeking to be a great man. He wanted the leaders to know that he did not propose church organization so that he would be put in charge of the movement. His desire was for the gospel to go to every man through every means possible.

A few days before he passed away, John Byington wrote in his diary "This is a day of comfort and peace. I have felt my sins were very many; have asked and found mercy of the Savior, and would declare His loving kindness to all." Byington was not seeking to be a great man but to be just before his God.

In 1950, at the General Conference session in San Francisco, California when the nominating committee selected the name of William H. Branson as world president of Seventh-day Adventists, he responded to the delegates. "I have always had very high ideals regarding the type of man who should stand as the leader of God's people. . . . I have never felt that I could personally measure up to that standard. . . . I have no natural abilities to carry such a task as you have asked me to carry. I see so much of weakness and faultiness in my life that I shrink from undertaking this holy task."

When Bob Spangler interviewed Elder Pierson after his health forced him to retire, Spangler asked Pierson if he was pleased to see the advance of the work during his tenure as president. Pierson replied, with tears in his eyes, "But the Lord isn't here yet, Bob, and anything short of that is not success." Years later, Robert Pearson died on his knees in Hawaii on Sabbath morning as he prepared to go to church and deliver a message.

Spicer and Figuhr regularly traveled in third class on public transportation to save on their travel budgets so that more preachers and teachers could be hired to spread the gospel. These officers were talented men who could have been highly successful as senators, statesmen, politicians and businessmen but the unction of the Holy Spirit had been placed upon them and they were Spirit-driven to give their all to preparing the world for Christ's return.

Because of their Spirit-driven leadership, Seventh-day Adventist Churches are springing up around the world today at the fastest rate in the denomination's history, with a new congregation opening its doors to worshipers every 3.58 hours, and a new member joining the church every 27 seconds.

A record 2,446 new churches opened in 2014, helping fuel the largest single-year increase in membership and bringing total Seventh-day Adventist membership to nearly 18.5 million.

It is my desire that these profiles, these short portraits for our busy lifestyles, will stir your heart as you see the true dedication of these officers who followed the leading of the Holy Spirit and guided the Adventist Church.

To share additional information or corrections please contact the author at
mdwilliams39@gmail.com

PRESIDENTS OF THE GENERAL CONFERENCE OF SEVENTH-DAY ADVENTISTS

1. John Byington 1863-1865
2. James White 1865-1867
3. J. N. Andrews 1867-1869
4. James White 1869-1871
5. George I. Butler........... 1871-1874
6. James White 1874-1880
7. George I. Butler........... 1880-1888
8. O. A. Olsen................. 1888-1897
9. G. A. Irwin 1897-1901
10. A. G. Daniells............ 1901-1922

11. W. A. Spicer 1922-1930
12. C. H. Watson 1930-1936
13. J. L. McElhany 1936-1950
14. W. H. Branson 1950-1954
15. R. R. Figuhr.............. 1954-1966
16. Robert H. Pierson...... 1966-1979
17. Neal C. Wilson 1979-1990
18. R. S. Folkenberg 1990-1999
19. Jan Paulsen 1999-2010
20. Ted N. C. Wilson....... 2010-

DID YOU KNOW THESE INTERESTING FACTS ABOUT
the Presidents of the Seventh-day Adventist Church?

Since the election of John Byington as our first General Conference president in 1863, a total of 17 men have held that office (including Byington). All but four have been born in the continental United States. O. A. Olsen (1888-1897) was born in Norway but brought to America by his parents when only five, while C. H. Watson (1930-1936), born in Australia, came to the States as an adult. Jan Paulsen was also born in Norway. Robert Folkenberg was born in Puerto Rico of American missionary parents.

John Byington was the only president born in the 1700s. He was born in 1798, a date which most Bible scholars believe was the beginning of the time of the end (1260 year prophecy, 538-1798).

James White served three non-consecutive terms and George Butler served two non-consecutive terms.

Perhaps the most unusual election took place in 1922. That year W. A. Spicer, who had been secretary of the General Conference from 1903-1922, became president. A. G. Daniells, who had been president for 21 years, was elected secretary. In exchanging positions, Elders Spicer and Daniells became the only men to serve as both president and secretary of the General Conference.

No General Conference treasurer has ever been elected president.

John Byington and James White were the only two presidents who never traveled outside of North America. Although Ellen White traveled extensively in Europe and Australia, James White had passed away before she made these trips.

Elder Olsen became president while not present at the session that elected him. He was preaching and evangelizing in Europe at the time. W. C. White, son of James and Ellen White, served as acting president for six months until Elder Olsen could finish up his work there and get back to the United States.

The General Conference chose James White as its first president, but he declined to serve because he had worked so hard for church organization. John Byington was then asked to serve in his place. James White later accepted three separate terms (1865-1867, 1869-1871, and 1874-1880).

A. G. Daniells (1901-1922) served as president for the longest period of time: twenty-one years; J. L. McElhany (1936-1950), the second longest for fourteen years. Two "firsts" served for only two years, the shortest time: our first president, John Byington (1863-1865); and our first missionary, John N. Andrews (1867-1869).

Two presidents were only 37 years old when elected; John N. Andrews and George I. Butler. Two presidents were elected at age 64; our first president, John Byington, and Jan Paulsen.

Two sets of presidents had the same birthday – *January 3:* J. L. McElhany, born *January 3,* 1880, and Robert H. Pierson born *January 3,* 1911 and *October 8*: John Byington born *October 8,* 1798, and Charles Watson born *October 8, 1877.* Two presidents died on the same day-*January 21*: William Branson, *January 21,* 1961 and Robert Pierson *January 21, 1989.*

Two deceased presidents are not buried in the United States. After Charles H. Watson retired he returned to his native Australia, where he later died and was buried. John Nevins Andrews passed away in Europe and is buried in Basel, Switzerland.

George Butler was converted to the Adventist faith by J. N. Andrews and later ordained to the ministry by James White. In 1910 another General Conference president, A. G. Daniells, ordained a future successor, young William H. Branson, to the ministry.

John Byington's oldest brother, Anson, operated a *documented* stop on the Underground Railroad. Elder John Byington, an abolitionist also, had hiding places built into the two churches he constructed and probably hid and assisted many slaves to freedom.

Neal Wilson, Robert Folkenberg, and Ted Wilson were all Adventist PKs (preacher's kids). Ted Wilson's grandfather was also a minister. Folkenberg is a fourth generation minister and his son Robert Jr. is a fifth generation minister. John Byington's father was an ordained itinerant Methodist minister.

George W. Brown was the only person nominated to the presidency who was non-Caucasian. Born in the Dominican Republic to an Antiguan father and Dominican mother (with a wife from Suriname), Brown declined the honor at the 1990 session in Indianapolis saying he was 66 and couldn't make the needed changes in one term and didn't feel his health and that of his family could support two terms.

At 6'5" Robert Folkenberg was the tallest president. Folkenberg also holds the distinction of being a licensed pilot and is qualified to fly jet planes and helicopters. He rides a motorcycle and has recorded 12 vocal solo records with Chapel Records.

Ted Wilson, PhD (New York University, New York, 1981) and Jan Paulsen, PhD (University of Tubingen) were the only two presidents to earn doctoral degrees. For the first time in the history of the Adventist Church, in addition to being ordained gospel ministers, all three of the executive officers elected in 2015 have earned doctorates. (PhDs).

Neal C. Wilson and Ted N. C. Wilson are the only father and son to have served as president. Nathaniel C. Wilson was the only minister to have both his son (Neal C. Wilson) and his grandson (Ted N.C. Wilson) serve as president of the General Conference.

Ellen G. White knew personally the first ten presidents. She spoke with, counseled, and wrote letters to them and their families. She died in 1915. Although the next ten presidents received no letters or personal advice from her, they all believed fully in her writings and teachings.

(Some of this information came from *Highly Committed, The Captivating Story of the Wilson Family and Their Impact on the Adventist Church*, DeWitt S. Williams, 2013, Teach Services, www.teachservices.com).

1. JOHN BYINGTON
May 21, 1863-May 17, 1865
(Two one-year terms)

Age when elected president: 64 years, 7 months
Church Membership When Elected: Estimated to be 3500
Secretary: Uriah Smith
Treasurer: Eli S. Walker

Born: October 8, 1798, in Hinesburg, Vermont
Died: January 7, 1887, in Battle Creek, Michigan. He was 88 years old.
Mother: Lucy Hinsdale Byington-(1759-1852)
Father: Justus Byington-(1763-1839); at the age of 16 Justus enlisted to fight in the Revolutionary War and received a pension from the government in later life. He became an itinerant Methodist Episcopal preacher. He was a delegate to the 1784 convention in Baltimore, Maryland, which organized the Methodist Church in America.
Siblings: John Byington was the sixth of ten children. When he traveled his father would leave John in charge of family worship because of his serious nature. His mother was very timid and reserved.
Wife: (1) Mary Priscilla Ferris- October 15, 1823, married in Monkton, Vermont, (Mary died while giving birth to her second child, Caroline).
(2) Catharine Newton- January 25, 1830, married in Charlotte, Vermont. Catharine was a 27-year-old Vermont school teacher and newly converted Methodist.
Children: By Mary Ferris: Julia (died in infancy) and Caroline Priscilla
By Catharine Newton: Laura, John Fletcher, Martha, Teresa, Luther Lee, William
Baptized: July 3, 1852, into the Adventist Church (at age 53) by G. W. Holt in the Grasse River near Bucks Bridge, New York.
Buried: Oak Hill Cemetery, Battle Creek, Michigan

Genesis. Abolitionist. Servant leadership.

The Adventist Church had its official, corporate beginning under John Byington's leadership. Only seventeen men have held this highest position of leadership and John Byington was the right man for the beginning. Byington was one of the oldest Adventist ministers in the denomination at that time. He outlived Joseph Bates and Hiram Edson. Because of his age and his kind leadership style he was often affectionately referred to as "Father Byington."

Tall, dignified, prudent, judicious, Byington was greatly respected for his unimpeachable integrity. Byington was very active in the Methodist Episcopal Church but he left it because it opposed his anti-slavery activities and he joined the new anti-slavery Wesleyan Methodist Connection. He helped erect a church and parsonage for both of these denominations in New York.

Byington heard William Miller preach in 1844 but was not ready to make a spiritual decision at that time. A friend gave him a copy of the *Advent Review and Sabbath Herald* which contained articles on the seventh-day Sabbath. After careful study of the Bible passages, he was convinced of the Bible Sabbath but was still reluctant to act on his conviction. He prayed to receive some unmistakable evidence and in one short week his youngest daughter sickened and died. After the death of his second daughter from smallpox three months later Byington, with his wife and two older children, was baptized into the fledgling Adventist movement at age 53 on July 3, 1852.

Byington became active in the Adventist Church as he had been in his other two denominations. He helped build an Adventist Church building in 1855 in Bucks Bridge (the Battle Creek, Michigan church was built in the same year but Byington's church opened and was dedicated earlier that year). At one time the Bucks Bridge church was believed to be the first church built by an Adventist congregation but recent evidence has been found that a church was built in Jackson, Michigan, in 1854.

Byington facilitated the opening of the first Adventist school in the denomination. His nineteen-year-old red-headed daughter Martha Byington (Amadon) began teaching 17 students in the parlor of a private home in Bucks Bridge, New York, in 1853. Martha became the first Adventist teacher in this school and the third year her brother John Fletcher Byington was the third teacher. From this embryonic beginning Adventist schools now belt the globe.

John Byington had the heavy responsibility of dealing with the problems that came with organizing a new church whose members were scattered like wandering sheep. Many Adventists had disconnected from their churches in 1844 awaiting the coming of the Lord. Since the Great Disappointment they didn't belong to any church. Many had become confused and fanatical. Byington sought them out, explained additional truth to them and connected them to the body of the Seventh-day Adventist Church.

There were also difficulties imposed on the Church by the Civil War. Byington, along with the other Adventist leaders, believed that slavery was a sin. In the same year that the church was organized (1863), Congress initiated the draft. Byington led the Church in raising money to purchase exemptions for its young men. At $300 per man, an exemption was beyond what most individuals could afford.

Byington was a cautious and deliberate man but he was very excited about nurturing new members. He was a revivalist and an exhorter, always seeking and encouraging members to be faithful. Byington esteemed James and Ellen White highly and knew them before he joined the church. At the request of the Whites he moved his family from Bucks Bridge, New York, to Newton, Michigan, (12 miles Southeast of Battle Creek) to do self-supporting preaching and revivals. He paid his own moving and travel expenses. He and his wife traveled so much by carriage (his horse was named Old Doll) and train that soon people started saying, "No one knows Michigan like John Byington." He often held revival meetings with J. N. Loughborough and baptized and nurtured many new members. His daughter Martha would sing and play the organ at his meetings.

He continued his close friendship with the Whites until his death. Byington retired to his Newton, Michigan, property after serving as president for two years and for more than twenty years thereafter he continued to preach, organize Sabbath schools, collect tithes and offerings and visit and encourage church members. His wife, Catharine, died suddenly of pneumonia when Byington was eighty-six after being sick only a week. John then moved in with his daughter in Battle Creek and died two years later. Until his death, driven by the dream of a soon-returning Savior, Father Byington wrote regular, brief encouraging letters of two or three paragraphs to his family, to new members and to the *Adventist Review* to share his abiding faith in Christ's gift of salvation.

"His last sickness was to him a time of deep searching of heart. Sometimes he experienced great depression, then there would be a rift in the clouds, and his joy would be almost ecstatic. Particularly did the Lord comfort him with very remarkable dreams. All who visited his room were exhorted to be living, earnest Christians; and especially did he warn the ministers, in view of the Judgment, to preach holiness of heart and life. He patiently bore his painful illness without murmuring, and often when praying that he might depart, he would add the petition, 'Thy will be done.' He chose the text for the funeral occasion, naming two brethren in the ministry whom he wished to speak on the passage: 'To him that overcometh will I grant to sit with me in my throne, even as I also overcame, and am set down with my Father in his throne.' Rev. 3: 21." G. W. Amadon, *9*, January 25, 1887, p.58.

More Interesting Facts

*The first John Byington came to America from Yorkshire, England, in 1696.

*Byington was the only Adventist president born in the 1700s.

*Byington and Jan Paulsen were the only presidents without a known middle name.

*Byington never received a salary while working for the church and supported himself by selling butter, produce from his farm and occasionally fitting dentures.

*Ellen White had a vision in Byington's house in Bucks Bridge (Potsdam township), New York in the early 1850s as they were having family worship which established Byington's belief in Ellen White as a prophet. Later Byington pitched a tent in one of his pastures and Ellen White had another vision in this tent about the Civil War.

*Byington's eyesight remained good as long as he lived. He read ten or more chapters from the Bible and portions of Mrs. White's *Testimonies* daily. His favorite subject was the Holy Spirit.

*John Byington's oldest brother Anson Byington operated a *documented* Underground Railroad station in Vermont. The churches and parsonages that John Byington built had secret hiding spaces. John Byington regularly entertained poor people and Negroes in his home and is said to have helped many runaway slaves on their way to freedom through the Underground Railroad at his Bucks Bridge farm in New York. His farm was near the St. Lawrence River and close to Canada. He highly esteemed Sojourner Truth who lived in nearby Battle Creek, Michigan.

* Sylvia Byington Nosworthy is a fifth generation Byington. Her parents were Paul and Ruth Nicola Nosworthy (an elementary teacher). Ruth's parents were Drs. Charles and Mary (Byington) Nicola who were put through medical school at the University of Michigan by Dr. Kellogg with the understanding that they would go into medical missionary work. They started the sanitarium at South Lancaster, Mass. Mary Byington was the daughter of John Fletcher Byington (son of John and Catharine Byington) and Martha Louisa Smith.

Slyvia started teaching in 1968 in academies in California; then 1974-78 taught English at Korean Union College (now University); in 1978 she went to Walla Walla College (now University) and in 2015 will complete her 37th year of teaching English at Walla Walla. She spends her summers in Michigan doing research in the Byington diaries and giving tours at the Historic Adventist Village in Battle Creek.

*Seventh and eighth generation Byingtons are still active in the Adventist Church today. Ellowyn Oster (a 4th generation missionary born in Iran) was baptized on the campus of Middle East College, Beirut, Lebanon, June 3, 1961, as generation Adventist. Her parents, Elder Kenneth and Dorothy Oster, were faculty there; her grandfather, Elder Frank Oster, was a pioneer missionary to Persia, beginning the work in Persia (Iran) in 1911; her great-grandfather, W.B. White, was a missionary in Africa and helped to organize the North Pacific Union and was president there; her great-great grandparents were Caroline Byington and Ambrose White and her great-great-great grandparents were John and Mary Byington, the GC president and his first wife. Ellowyn Oster's daughter Yvonne Kroehler of Michigan today is a seventh generation Adventist and she home schools her three children (Ellyanna, Jeffrey and Aden Kroehler) who are eighth generation Adventists. Ellowyn's brother, Dr. Cyrus Oster (also born in Iran) is a sixth generation Adventist and a dentist in California. His unmarried seventh generation son is also a dentist who just returned from a stint of mission service in Palau.

Father John Byington, as he was affectionately called, and is typically remembered.

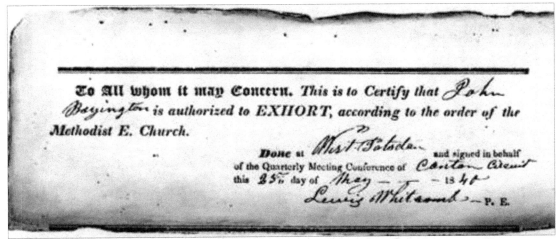

The authorization from the Methodist Church for John Byington to "exhort," or be a lay preacher.
As a circuit riding pastor, he worked to support himself, rode, and preached, visiting homes of the needy in his district.

(Left) Mrs. Catharine Byington as a young lady.
(Right) Mrs. Catharine Byington as an elderly lady.

(Left) During the Civil War Sojourner Truth raised food and clothing contributions for black regiments,
and met Abraham Lincoln at the White House in 1864. She is buried near John Byington.
(Right) Sojourner Truth (1797-1883) was born into slavery in New York as Isabella Baumfree. In 1843, she took the name
Sojourner Truth and became a traveling preacher (the meaning of her new name). In the late 1840s she connected with the
abolitionist movement and the Millerites and in 1850 she began speaking on woman's suffrage. Her most famous speech,
"Ain't I a Woman?" was given in 1851 at a women's rights convention in Ohio.

18

The Amadon residence on Hill Street, Battle Creek, Michigan. John Byington
spent the last few years of his life with his daughter in this home.

A stone marker showing the spot of the first Adventist Church in 1855 and school in 1853 in Bucks Bridge, New York.

George W. Amadon, employee of the Review and Herald press for 50 years, with his wife, Martha Byington, a daughter of John Byington.

Martha Byington Amadon on her 100th birthday, March 28, 1934. She was nearly 103 when she died.

John Byington is being congratulated by James White and J. M. Aldrich, as president of the General Conference session that elected him. Seated in the background is Joseph Bates. The occasion is the founding meeting of the Adventist Church, May 1863. From a painting by Vernon Nye in the *Adventist Review* (December 6, 1979).

The grave site of John Byington in Battle Creek, Michigan.

Sixth and seventh generation Byingtons who are all dentists. Dr. Cyrus Oster (back right) and his son, Nathan (front left). His brother Don Oster's two sons are also dentists: Cyrus G. (back left) and Nick Oster (front right).

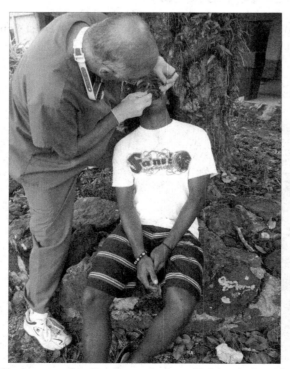

(Left) Sixth generation Dr. Cyrus Oster on Palau mission trip doing some screening on a patient. His son, Dr. Nathan Oster (LLU class of 2014) helped organize the trip. The group saw 1000 patients that week and fixed hundreds of teeth.
(Right) Dr. Cyrus Oster and his son Captain Nathan Oster, sixth and seventh generation Byingtons.

Sylvia Byington Nosworthy holds a portrait of her great-great-grandfather John Byington. Sylvia works at the Historic Adventist Village in Battle Creek, Michigan during the summers (photo by Krystal Eskildsen) and at Walla Walla University during the school year.

A group from Oakwood College visiting the gravesite of Sojourner Truth at Oak Hill Cemetery in Battle Creek, Michigan. Sojourner enjoyed the friendship of John Byington, Dr. John Harvey Kellogg and other prominent Adventists. Sojourner died on November 26, 1883 and her funeral, attended by approximately a thousand people, was held in the Congregational Church in downtown Battle Creek.

The Hardy family is considered to be the first baptized African-American family in the Adventist Church. In October of 1857, meetings conducted by Joseph Frisbie, John Byington, and James and Ellen White were held in Caledonia, Michigan. Byington records in his diary that he spent the night with the Hardy family on the day of baptism. Eliza was baptized that day, then her husband William pulled out of the Free Will Baptist Church and cast his lot with the Adventists. Years later, William was elected elder of the church and their children grew up Adventists. Pictured here is Eliza and Williams' oldest son, Eugene Hardy, who studied law and was a music teacher.

Seventh and eighth generation Byingtons. Ellyanna, JP, and Aden doing their schoolwork with their mother Yvonne Kroehler.

The Founding Session
May 20-21, 1863

The decade following the disappointment was a time of chaos in Adventist circles. William Miller and his associates never intended to create a new church. They expected Christ to return to the earth and were confused when He didn't. Most had been cast out of their mother churches for their beliefs. The experience prejudiced them against church organization. After the Disappointment their faith was torn by diverse teachings and irreconcilable leaders. At the same time their bias against organization continued and prevented any definite unity.

Sabbath-keeping spread slowly among the first-day Adventists. Rachel Oakes Preston, William and Cyrus Farnsworth, Joseph Bates, John Andrews and a few others began keeping the Sabbath. The Holy Spirit impressed upon sincere students of the Bible that the Ten Commandments, including the Bible Sabbath, were still God's plan for all ages. The Sabbath truth spread. In the 1850s, groups of Sabbath-keeping believers were scattered throughout New England and as far west as Iowa and Wisconsin. In the early 1860s state conferences were established leading to the organization of the Church in 1863.

In *Testimonies to Ministers and Gospel Workers*, page 26, we find Mrs. White's statement on church organization. "As our numbers increased, it was evident that without some form of organization there would be great confusion, and the work would not be carried forward successfully. To provide for the support of the ministry, for carrying the work in new fields, for protecting both the churches and the ministry from unworthy members, for holding church property, for the publication of the truth through the press, and for many other objects, organization was indispensable."

Wednesday evening, May 20, 1863, at 6:00 p.m. twenty-one men assembled in the little Battle Creek, Michigan, church. The organizational meeting of the Seventh-day Adventist Church was about to take Adventist Church should have been caught in the search and find but just in case I have highlighted it place. The meeting had been called by the delegates of the Michigan Conference.

The meeting was temporarily organized that evening by choosing Jotham M. Aldrich, chairman, and Uriah Smith, secretary. After singing hymn number 233 from their hymnal (entitled *Hymns for Those Who Keep the Commandments of God, and the Faith of Jesus*) and offering a prayer for guidance, a committee was appointed to examine the credentials of the elected state delegates who were present. Not much more happened that night.

When the meeting opened at 9 o'clock Thursday morning twenty delegates were officially voted in from their respective states (Uriah Smith, a layman at that time, was also present, making the twenty-first person. He did not list himself as a delegate but he signed the minutes each day as being the secretary of the Conference). The credentials from the six states were examined and they were considered bona fide state representatives. There were no women and three laymen.

From **New York (4)**: John N. Andrews, Jotham Aldrich, Nathan Fuller, and Charles Taylor.
Ohio (2): I. N. Van Gorder and H. F. Baker. (No pictures are available.)
Michigan (10): James White, Joseph Bates, Joseph Waggoner, John Byington, John Loughborough, *Moses Hull, Meritt Cornell, Russell Lawrence, and a layman, W. S. Higley, Jr. James Harvey, also a layman, from **Indiana**, was included in and met with this group.
Wisconsin (1): Isaac Sanborn.
****Iowa (2)**: Benjamin Snook and William H. Brinkerhoff.
Minnesota (1): Washington Morse.

Their assignment was to adopt a constitution and elect officers for the new General Conference of Seventh-day Adventists. The estimated membership of the Church at that time was 3,500 with twenty two ministers and eight licentiates.

These are the steps leading up to this organizational meeting. About three years earlier Elder James White had printed an article in the *Advent Review and Sabbath Herald*, February 23, 1860, issue suggesting that there was a great need for organization. A conference convened in Battle Creek, Michigan, September 28 to October 1, 1860, to consider the question of organization. Elder White argued that for growth and advancement it was necessary to legally organize the publishing work and they must find a way to hold church property. Many present felt that the group became Babylon the moment men organized it. Others were also convinced that Jesus' return was no more than months, or at most, a few years away. These groups opposed organization. On October 1, 1860, this meeting, chaired by Joseph Bates, adopted the name Seventh-day Adventists.

A committee of five was then appointed to carry out the project of incorporating the publishing business. On May 3, 1861, the Seventh-day Adventist Publishing Association was organized and incorporated under the laws of Michigan, the first legal body of the denomination.

At the time there were no laws in Michigan providing for nonprofit-sharing corporations. Owing very largely to the Advent enterprises, especially the sanitarium, such a law was later enacted, and the publishing association was reorganized on that basis. James White transferred the property to this association on June 2, 1861.

On October 5 and 6, 1861, the churches in the state of Michigan (including several churches in northern Indiana) organized under the name of the Michigan Conference of Seventh-day Adventists, the first conference to be organized among Seventh-day Adventists. Churches were to have no creed but the Bible and in each congregation members would sign a covenant that they were associating together under the name of Seventh-day Adventists. Within a year five other state conferences were organized.

At the second meeting of the Michigan Conference (October, 1862) it was moved that the next Michigan Conference should be held at Battle Creek and, most importantly, that they should through the *Review* "invite the several State Conferences to meet with us, by delegate."

The founding session venue was the second church building constructed in Battle Creek. The first little church building had been constructed in 1855 with a seating capacity of forty persons. In 1857, with the growth of the publishing house and the moves made there by its employees, a new, much larger meeting house was constructed. The second church building had been erected at a cost of $881 and measured 28 feet by 42 feet. It had separate entrances at the front for men and for women.

The Constitution committee, headed by John Andrews, brought in a constitution with nine articles which was adopted. In the Thursday afternoon session the committee on nominations brought in the report of the officers: (James White's name was presented first for president but he refused to accept. After great discussion on this his resignation was finally accepted); John Byington, president; Uriah Smith, secretary; and Eli Walker, treasurer (who probably was not present at the meeting). Of the three officers chosen, Byington was the only ordained minister at the time. Uriah Smith would be ordained in 1874. The Executive Committee was to operate the church between sessions and was composed of: James White, John Byington, John Loughborough, John Andrews, and George Amadon.

Uriah Smith details the wonderful spirit of unity, joy, peace and love that pervaded the entire organizational meeting from start to finish. "We hardly know what feature of the joyful occasion to notice first. We can say to the readers of the *Review*, Think of everything good that has been written of every previous meeting, and apply it to this. All this would be true, and more than this. Perhaps no previous meeting that we have ever enjoyed, was characterized by such unity of feeling and harmony of sentiment. In all the important steps taken at this Conference, in the organization of a General Conference, and the further perfecting of State Conferences, defining the authority of each, and the important duties belonging to their various officers, there was not a dissenting voice, and we may reasonably doubt if there was even a dissenting thought. Such union, on such points, affords the strongest grounds of hope for the immediate advancement of the cause, and its future glorious prosperity and triumph." *Advent Review and Sabbath Herald*, May 26, 1863, p. 4.

On Friday the large Michigan evangelistic tent was erected on the grass not far from the office. Members from all over arrived and were treated to a feast of spirit-filled preaching by leading ministers that Sabbath evening, all during Sabbath day and Sunday morning. At the close of the meetings eight people were baptized. The organizational meeting of the Adventist Church had been a great and wonderful occasion!

*Within a few months of this founding meeting Hull would break ties with Adventists. Hull had been a Sundaykeeping Adventist for about six years (c.1851 to 1857) before he joined the Sabbathkeeping Adventists. He was ordained to the ministry by first-day Adventists when he was 18 but was ordained by James White again in 1858. Hull was an outstanding preacher and evangelist but began debating spiritualists in 1862. The debates seemed to confuse Hull. One part of the vision Mrs. White had in Otsego, Michigan, on June 5, 1863, was for Moses Hull. She counseled him against undue familiarity with women and warned him against accepting flattery.

Hull left the Adventist Church and became an active missionary for spiritualism in spite of the prayers of James and Ellen White and the other leaders of the Adventist Church.

**Snook and Brinkerhoff, the representatives from Iowa, had doubts and conflicts related to Ellen White and her visions, James White and the Battle Creek church. They began to express their opinions and doubts openly. After being sternly reproved they sent letters of repentance and confession to the *Review* which were published. Toward the end of 1865 they relapsed and in spite of their former confessions, went from church to church in Iowa spreading doubt about the Adventist Church, its leaders and its doctrines.

The disaffected group formed what came to be known as the Marion Party, named after Marion, Iowa, where the movement was headquartered. They later merged with the remnants of the Gilbert Cranmer group. Snook and Brinkerhoff published a booklet entitled *The Visions of E. G. White, Not of God*. Snook soon left the group and became a Universalist minister. Brinkerhoff also left and returned to his former profession of a lawyer.

The merged group took the name Church of God (Seventh Day) or simply CoG7 today, and is presently headquartered in Denver, Colorado. As of 2012, the Church of God (Seventh Day) has over 200 congregations in the United States and Canada and the worldwide membership in its International Ministerial Congress is over 200,000 members, with affiliated ministries in more than 40 countries.

John Byington, President; Uriah Smith, Secretary; Eli Walker, Treasurer-
the first officers of the General Conference of Seventh-day Adventists.

New York
J. N. Andrews

New York
Jotham Aldrich

New York
Nathan Fuller

New York
Charles Taylor

Michigan
Joseph Bates

Michigan
Joseph Waggoner

Michigan
John Loughborough

Michigan
Moses Hull

Michigan
Merritt Cornell

Michigan
Russell Lawrence

Wisconsin
Isaac Sanborn

Indiana
James Harvey

Iowa
Benjamin Snook

Iowa
William Brinkerhoff

Minnesota
Washington Morse

Michigan
James White

CONSTITUTION OF GENERAL CONFERENCE.

For the purpose of securing unity and efficiency in labor, and promoting the general interests of the cause of present truth, and of perfecting the organization of the Seventh-day Adventists, we, the delegates from the several State Conferences, hereby proceed to organize a General Conference, and adopt the following constitution for the government thereof:

Article I. This Conference shall be called the General Conference of Seventh-day Adventists.

Art. II. The officers of this Conference shall be a President, Secretary, Treasurer, and an Executive Committee of three, of whom the President shall be one.

Art. III. The duties of the President and Secretary shall be such respectively as usually pertain to those offices.

Art. IV. It shall be the duty of the Treasurer to receive and disburse means under the direction of the Executive Committee, and keep an account of the same, and make a full report thereof to the regular meetings of the Conference.

Art. V. Section 1. It shall be the duty of the Executive Committee to take the general supervision of all ministerial labor, and see that the same is properly distributed ; and they shall take the special supervision of all missionary labor, and as a missionary board shall have the power to decide where such labor is needed, and who shall go as missionaries to perform the same.

Sec. 2. Means for missionary operations may be received by donation from State Conferences, churches, or individuals ; and the Committee are authorized to call for means when needed.

Constitution 1

Sec. 3. When any State Conference desires ministerial labor from a minister not a resident within the bounds of such Conference, their request shall be made to the General Conference Executive Committee, and ministers sent by said Committee shall be considered under the jurisdiction of the Conf. Committee of such State: *Provided*, 1. That if such minister consider the State Committee inefficient, or their action so far wrong as to render his labor ineffectual, he may appeal to the General Conference Executive Committee: *Provided*, 2. That if such State Committee consider such minister inefficient they may appeal to the General Conference Committee, who shall decide on the matter of complaint, and take such action as they may think proper.

Art. VI. Each State Conference shall be entitled to one delegate in the General Conference, and one additional delegate for every twenty delegates in the State Conference, such delegates to the General Conference to be chosen by the State Conferences or their Committees: *Provided*, That the delegates to such State Conferences be elected according to the following ratio, to wit: Each church to the number of twenty members or under shall be entitled to one delegate, and one delegate for every additional fifteen members.

Art. VII. The officers shall hold their offices for the term of one year, and shall be elected at the regular meetings of the Conference.

Art. VIII. Sec. 1. The regular meetings of the Conference shall be held annually, and the time and place of holding the same shall be determined by the Executive Committee, by whom due notice thereof shall be given through the Review.

Sec. 2. Special meetings may be called at the option of the Committee.

Art. IX. This constitution may be altered or amended by a two-third's vote of the delegates present at any regular meeting: *Provided*, That any proposed amendment shall be communicated to the Executive Committee, and notice thereof given by them in their call for the meeting of the Conference.

Report of General Conference of Seventh-day Adventists.

THE General Conference of S. D. Adventists convened according to appointment at Battle Creek, Mich., May 20, at 6 o'clock P. M. The meeting was temporarily organized by choosing J. M. Aldrich, chairman, and U. Smith, secretary. The Conference was then opened by singing the hymn on page 233, and prayer by Bro. Snook. A committee to receive and judge of the credentials of delegates being called for, it was

Voted, That we have a committee of three on credentials.

The following brethren were thereupon chosen as that committee: Eld. J. N. Loughborough, of Mich., C. O. Taylor, of N. Y., and Isaac Sanborn, of Wis.

The remainder of this session was occupied in the presentation of credentials to the committee, and the meeting adjourned to the following morning, May 21, at 9 o'clock.

In the morning session, the committee announced the following brethren as the duly elected delegates from their respective States: From New York, Brn. J. N. Andrews, N. Fuller, C. O. Taylor, and J. M. Aldrich. From Ohio, I. N. Van Gorder. From Michigan, the ministers present from that State, namely, Brn. White, Bates, Waggoner, Byington, Loughborough, Hull, Cornell, and Lawrence, with a lay representation of Brn. James Harvey, of North Liberty, Ind., and Wm. S. Higley, jr., of Lapeer, Mich. From Wisconsin, Isaac Sanborn. From Iowa, Brn. B. F. Snook, and W. H. Brinkerhoof. From Minnesota, Washington Morse.

The report of the committee was accepted.

Voted, That Bro. H. F. Baker be received as an additional delegate from Ohio.

The following brethren were then appointed a committee to draft a constitution and by-laws for the government of this Conference: Brn. J. N. Andrews, N. Fuller, I. Sanborn, W. Morse, H. F. Baker, B. F. Snook, J. H. Waggoner, and J. N. Loughborough. After due deliberation the committee presented the following constitution for the consideration of the Conference:

(Left) Constitution 2
(Right) Report

2.4.6. JAMES SPRINGER WHITE
First Time: May 17, 1865-May 14-1867
Second Time: May 18, 1869-December 29, 1871
Third Time: August 10, 1874-October 6-1880
(Total of 10 one-year terms)

Age When First Elected President: 43 years old
Second time: 47 years old
Third time: 53 years old
Church Membership: First church census in 1867 showed: **4320 members**
Secretaries: Uriah Smith, C. W. Stone
Treasurers: I. D. Van Horn, E. S. Walker, G. H. Bell, Mrs. A. P. Van Horn, Harmon Lindsay

Born: August 4, 1821, in Palmyra, Maine.
Died: August 6, 1881, in Battle Creek, Michigan; two days after his 60th birthday.
Mother: Elizabeth "Betsey" Jewett White (granddaughter of Dr. Samuel Shepard, a Baptist preacher). Of his mother, James White said that she was "one of the sweetest and best women that lived."
Father: "Deacon" John White, a farmer and music teacher in Maine.
Siblings: The fifth of nine children- James was right in the middle, four younger and four older.
Wife: Married Ellen G. Harmon, August 30, 1846, before the Justice of the Peace in Portland, Maine. James was twenty five years old and Ellen was eighteen years old.
Children: 1. Henry Nichols White (August 26, 1847-December 8, 1863) 16 years old
        2. James Edson White (July 28-1849-June 3, 1928) 78 years old
        3. William (Willie) Clarence White (August 29, 1854-August 31, 1937) 83 years old
        4. John Herbert White (September 20-December 14, 1860)
Church Affiliation of Parents: Christian Connexion Church
Baptized: At age 15 into the Christian Connexion Church
Ordained: As a minister of the Christian Connexion Church in April, 1843 at age 22
Buried: In the White family lot in the Oak Hill Cemetery in Battle Creek, Michigan, close to his father and mother and his two sons, Henry and John Herbert White.

Visionary. Indefatigable. Co-Founder.

James White, the founder and first editor of the *Review*, was a towering figure in early Adventist history. With his wife, Ellen G. White and Joseph Bates, he is considered to be the co-founder of the Seventh-day Adventist Church. He was the only person to serve as General Conference president three separate times.

Weak and sickly as a child, he first attended school at the age of sixteen. He began teaching school at age nineteen. In September, 1842, he heard William Miller speak about the return of the Lord at an Adventist camp meeting in Maine. He was so impressed that he cut short his anticipated career as a schoolteacher, purchased a prophetic chart and an assortment of publications to study.

Though only a youth of twenty-one, he began preaching the warning message to his pupils, their parents, and anyone else who would listen. It is reported that he was responsible for 1000 conversions before the Great Disappointment of 1844.

James and Ellen White began married life without money, without jobs, and in poor health. Ellen was frail, weighing about 80 pounds and suffering from a childhood injury. James had a continually upset stomach (dyspepsia). But they shared the same burning desire to prepare others for the second coming of Christ.

James and Ellen White made an effective team. James was wholly dedicated to preaching the Sabbath truth and had remarkable foresight and business acumen. After two visions from Ellen White urging him to publish the Advent message, James began to print a little paper. With his three shilling pocket Bible, *Cruden's Concordance*, and a raggedy dictionary he began preparing articles for the paper which he called *The Present Truth*. The first issue came from the press in late July, 1849. During the next sixteen months he published eleven issues. In November, 1850, at a conference held in Paris, Maine, the name of the paper was changed to *The Second Advent Review and Sabbath Herald*.

James and Ellen White suffered a great deal from poverty and even lacked proper food, but the paper went out every two weeks. It was free to anyone who wanted it but they gladly accepted donations to sustain its publication. In 1852, the paper moved to Rochester, New York. Believers there worked together to buy a printing press and other equipment. Elder White next published a monthly journal for the young people of the Sabbath-keeping Rochester Adventist families called *The Youth's Instructor*.

In 1855 members in Michigan requested that he move the publishing work to Battle Creek and they promised to provide a publishing house. Within a decade after the move to Michigan the Review and Herald office under James White's leadership was the largest and best-equipped publishing facility in the state of Michigan. It was White's requests for help to operate the publishing business that led the other Adventist leaders to think about organizing the work. Subsequently, the publishing work was organized, the name Seventh-day Adventists was selected and the Michigan Conference was formed.

On May 21, 1863, when the General Conference was organized James White was unanimously elected to be the first president. He declined lest some should say that his concerted appeals for church organization were for the creation of an office for himself. Two years later he was elected again after Byington had finished his two terms. He declined again saying that his work load at the *Review* was too much. The denomination released him from his duties as chief editor of the *Review* and White accepted and carried the responsibility of president on three separate occasions and served as president until 1880, a few months before his death.

Elder White dreamed of a publishing house on the West Coast that would have an evangelistic thrust. In June, 1874, the *Signs of the Times* was founded and two years later the Pacific Press was established in Oakland, California. This publishing house soon became the largest and best-equipped printing operation in the West.

Seeing the need for a large auditorium in Battle Creek in which to hold general meetings, James White led out in 1878 in raising funds for the Battle Creek Tabernacle. It became known as the "Dime Tabernacle," because White called for every church member to contribute a dime a month towards its financing. The Tabernacle with its three vestries and gallery opened could seat 3200 people.

James White came from a musical family. His father taught vocal music, and his sisters were talented singers. Before his marriage, James, with his family, were forced by a storm to take shelter in a hotel during a trip to Eastern Maine. The storm forced many other people to spend the night in the same hotel. The Whites spent the evening entertaining a large crowd with religious songs. The hotel guests enjoyed the music so much that the owner refused to charge the Whites for rooms stating that they had already paid their bill by their music. Often when Elder White had to preach he would enter an auditorium singing in his strong voice as he came down the aisle beating time on his Bible. The congregation would join in singing with him and a deep spiritual mood would spread over the audience in anticipation of his sermon.

In 1849 Elder White compiled a small book of hymns with just words and no musical notes for the use of the early Adventists. The tiny book, 3.5" x 5" with 48 pages, had a big title: *Hymns for God's Peculiar People That Keep the Commandments of God and the Faith of Jesus*. In 1878 his son, James Edson, produced the first denominational songbook with musical notes called *The Song Anchor*. In 1886, he collaborated with his cousin, Frank Belden, in producing *Joyful Greetings for the Sabbath School*.

James suffered three paralytic strokes from overwork. Ellen had several visions telling him that he must share his workload with younger men but he constantly taxed his mental and physical reserves. He became ill with fever and chills from malaria during the summer of 1881. He was at his home preparing to write on the subject of redemption. He was rushed to the Battle Creek Sanitarium and placed under the care of Dr. Kellogg but he failed to respond to his best treatment. On Sabbath afternoon, August 6, the tireless church leader ceased his work forever. The funeral in the Battle Creek Tabernacle was attended by 2500 Adventists and citizens of the city.

More Interesting Facts

*James White heard William Miller preach in 1842. He resigned from school, bought a prophetic chart and prepared seven sermons and started preaching. Sixty repentant people requested prayer and indicated a desire for baptism at the end of his meetings.

*During the winter months of 1842-1843 James White's preaching influenced more than one thousand people to accept Christ and the teaching of Christ's soon second coming.

*James was sickly with eye problems as a young boy. He did not go to school until he was sixteen. At nineteen, he entered an academy at St. Albans, Maine, studied eighteen hours a day and in three months received his certificate to teach. An additional four and a half months of school at Reedfield, Maine, completed all the formal schooling he would ever have.

*Two of their four sons died while young. Henry, the oldest, died of pneumonia at age 16. Herbert, the youngest, died before the age of three months. The remaining two sons, James Edson and William C., became ordained ministers. Edson White had no children but W.C. White gave the Whites seven grandchildren.

*James White was a man of prayer. He and Ellen reserved a bit of woods on the corner of their first purchased Battle Creek lot so they could have a quiet spot in which to retire for prayer.

*It was James White's vision that led to the establishment of the first Adventist health care institution which, under the direction of Dr. John Harvey Kellogg, developed into the world-famous Battle Creek Sanitarium.

The White family c.1865. Willie (left) and Edson.

Adelia Patten (Van Horn) lived with James and Ellen White as a young lady.
She served as a literary assistant to Ellen White later. She poses with the White family.

(Left) Edson and Willie White.
(Right) Ellen and her twin sister, Elizabeth (Harmon Bangs). The twins were the last of eight children of Robert and Eunice Harmon, born near Gorham, Maine. "Lizzie" died fourteen years before Ellen and it is not clear whether she ever became a Seventh-day Adventist.

(Left) "Deacon" John White, the father of James White.
(Right) Elizabeth "Betsey" White, mother of James White.

James and his wife, Ellen White.

The White Brothers, Henry (left), Edson (middle) and Willie (right), around 1862: There was a fourth son, John Herbert, born Sept. 20, 1860. He died that same year, in December. Henry died December 8, 1863, at the age of sixteen years, three months. Edson and Willie lived to old age.

James White's grave, Oak Hill Cemetery, Battle Creek, Michigan.

Arthur and Frieda White. Arthur was the grandson of James and Ellen and the third son of William C. White. Arthur was almost eight years old when his grandmother, Ellen G. White died. After the death of W. C. White in 1937 the Ellen G. White Estate was moved to the General Conference in Washington, and Arthur was appointed secretary (director) of the board of trustees. He served in this position for more than 40 years and traveled around the world giving workshops and seminars on Ellen White and her prophetic gift. Here with sons William, James, and Arthur H.

(Left) James Edson White, the second son. He mastered the printing trade. In 1893 Edson read a copy of Ellen White's *Our Duty to the Colored People* and he built a missionary steamboat, the *Morning Star,* at Allegan, Michigan, in 1894, at a cost of $3700.

(Right) *The Southern Work* was a compilation of several articles written by Ellen White which sought to stir the church to evangelistic and educational efforts on behalf of Southern Blacks. Edson White compiled them and used them as his marching orders for work in the South.

The Morning Star boat

Henry and Herbert White with Arthur.

On June 12, 1905, Mrs. White and her son Willie visited Loma Linda, California for the first time. She knew it to be the location she had seen in a dream four years earlier and the land was purchased for Loma Linda University. The sculpture was made by Victor Issa. This visionary guidance has been a blessing to the Adventist Church.

Ellen White's grave at funeral. She is buried next to James in the Oak Hill Cemetery, Battle Creek, Michigan

(Left) Herbert and Henry White, twins, 1911, age 14 (and later) 86. Ellen White had a twin sister and her son,
Willie (W.C.) had twin sons born in Tasmania in April, 1896.
(Right) Herbert and Henry, twin sons of William Clarence White and his wife, May Lacey White.
They were born while Elder White was helping his mother in Australia.

Scenes from Willie (W. C.) White's life

THE PRESENT TRUTH.

PUBLISHED SEMI-MONTHLY—BY JAMES WHITE.

| Vol. 1. | MIDDLETOWN, CONN, JULY, 1849. | No. 1. |

"The secret of the Lord is with them that fear him; and he will shew them his covenant."—Ps. xxv. 14.

The first issue of *The Present Truth* published July, 1849.

James White carrying his papers to the printers in his carpetbag.

Arthur White standing next to a tower of Ellen G. White books-70 in all-stacked on the floor of the White Estate vault in Washington D. C. Included are the regular current volumes (52); *SDA Bible Commentary*, Vol. 7a, Ellen G. Whtie Comments (1 volume); The photo was taken by J. Byron Logan.

3. JOHN NEVINS ANDREWS
May 14, 1867-May 18, 1869
(2 one-year terms)

Age when Elected President: 37 years, 9 months
Church Membership When Elected: 4320
Secretary: Uriah Smith
Treasurer: I. D. Van Horn, J. N. Loughborough

Born: July 22, 1829, in Poland, Maine
Died: October 21, 1883, Basel, Switzerland. He was 54 years old.
Mother: Sarah Pottle Andrews (1803-1899)
Father: Edward Andrews (1798-1865), a farmer.
Sibling: William Andrews
Wife: Married October 29, 1856, to Angeline S. Stevens in Waukon, Iowa. Angeline died March 18, 1872, of a stroke at age 48. Angeline's sister, Harriet Stevens, was the wife of Uriah Smith.
Children: Charles Melville (1857-1927)
Mary Frances (1861-1878). She contracted tuberculosis in Switzerland and returned to the States to be treated at the Battle Creek Sanitarium. She is buried in Mount Hope Cemetery in Rochester, New York, next to her mother and sister, Carrie.
3rd child died after four days in 1863 in New York
4th child, Carrie Matilda (1864-1865) died of dysentery when 13 months old
Ordained: 1853 at age 24 by James White
Buried: Basel, Switzerland

Brilliant scholar. First missionary. Linguist.

At thirteen John Andrews accepted Christ as his Savior and became interested in the Millerite movement. As a lad of fifteen, John shared with his parents and scores of thousands of other believers the keen disappointment of October 22, 1844, the day they predicted that Christ would return from heaven. In 1845 at age fifteen young Andrews read an article written by a Seventh Day Baptist advocating the seventh day of the week as the Sabbath. He decided to keep the Sabbath with the young lady, Marian Stowell, and her brother, Oswald, who had read the tract and kept the Sabbath the week before in secret. The youths took the tract to their parents who read it and were also convinced of the Sabbath. Soon the Stowell and the Andrews families were keeping the Sabbath together.

After the Great Disappointment of 1844 a group of believers in Maine became depressed and fanatical. Some advocated a "no work" position. They taught that they were in the millennium, the thousand years of peace and bliss that some people believed would take place on earth. The parents of John Andrews got caught up in this kind of fanaticism. In September 1849, James and Ellen White visited Paris, Maine, and called a meeting to talk with these estranged believers. The Andrews family and the Cyprian Stevens family shared this belief and were in the specially called meeting. Twenty-year-old John Nevins Andrews also attended the meeting and was fascinated by what he heard and saw. He made a decision to stand for what the Bible taught.

One year later John was in the gospel ministry. John's uncle Charles (his father's brother) was a man of political importance in Maine, a United States congressman. Uncle Charles kept encouraging John to enter politics but John Andrews now had his mind set on ministry. The Andrews family had a very large house in Paris, Maine, which accommodated many visitors. James and Ellen White lived with John's parents from

November 1850, until June 1851. After John married Angeline Stevens he moved to Iowa and wrote the first edition of his best-known work, *The History of the Sabbath and the First Day of the Week.*

Andrews was chosen as the denominational representative to the provost marshal general in Washington, D.C. to acquire recognition for Adventists as noncombatants. When the Civil War started in 1861 the Adventist Church was not yet organized. As the draft was enforced the leaders recognized that they needed to have an exemption for Adventist young men. Andrews wrote a recommendation regarding the proper course Seventh-day Adventist young men of draft age should follow and went to Washington to contact officials in the War Department to request that Adventist soldiers be conscientious objectors.

He served as the third president of the General Conference and immediately afterwards as editor of the *Advent Review and Sabbath Herald.* During his presidency the church, located entirely in the northern states, began its westward expansion. Andrews encouraged Elders John Loughborough and Daniel T. Bourdeau, two of the church's most seasoned evangelists to move westward. They sailed to California in 1868 by way of the Isthmus of Panama.

Under Andrews' leadership the church organized its first official camp meeting. Twenty-two families pitched their tents in a sugar maple grove on E. H. Root's farm near Wright, Michigan. Originally a frontier phenomenon, the camp meeting was declining with increasing urbanization. Through Andrews' influence, this religious convocation was adopted by the church whose rural ideals resisted urban encroachment. Though Andrews advocated the camp meeting as an evangelistic tool, it eventually became an annual retreat focusing on renewal among church members after the 1920's.

Andrews did extensive research on various doctrines of the young church and it was his research that convinced the denomination to start observing the Sabbath from Friday at sunset. Joseph Bates had believed that the Sabbath began at six o'clock on Friday evening and lasted until six o'clock on Saturday. Andrews also led out in the study to determine what the Bible teaches regarding the support of the ministry and the result was the emergence of The Systematic Benevolence Plan which in 1877 became the tithing plan. The Battle Creek church was quick to adopt this plan but it was slow to spread to all the other churches.

Andrews's wife, Angeline, died from a stroke in 1872. When the leaders received an urgent request from Switzerland for someone to teach them more about Adventist's beliefs they selected Andrews. They considered him to be the most brilliant young theologian they had and a man with pastoral experience who would rely on God for leading. On September 15, 1874, Andrews and his two teenage children, Charles and Mary, left the United States as the first official Adventist missionaries to Europe. Mrs. White said that the church had sent the "ablest man in all our ranks." (The church had only twenty-eight ordained ministers at that time).

A month later he arrived in Neuchatel, Switzerland, and began earnest study of the French language. After a year he had contacted seventy-five Sabbath observers in Europe. He preached wherever there was an interest. One night he arrived at a meeting in a hotel and saw four rows of tables extending the entire length of the hall. Each table had men sitting smoking from pipes about four feet long and drinking from glasses of beer. Andrews admitted that although they listened attentively it was a strange environment.

By 1876 he had moved to Basel, Switzerland, and set up an office in one of the rooms in his house. He began printing the first Adventist periodical in French: *Les Signes des Temps (Signs of the Times).* By 1878 he was able to report Sabbath keepers in England, Scotland, Ireland, Norway, Sweden, Denmark, Holland, Alsace, Germany, France, Italy, and Egypt. Mary, his fifteen-year-old daughter, was able to speak French fluently and was able to catch grammatical errors that escaped the Swiss help.

But Mary became sick with tuberculosis. When Andrews returned to Battle Creek for the General Conference session he took her with him so he could have Dr. Kellogg look at her and hopefully cure her. But two months later, November 27, 1878, Mary died. Mrs. White wrote him, "In my last vision, I saw you. Your head was inclined toward the earth. . . .I saw the Lord looking upon you full of love and compassion. I saw the coming of Him who is to give life to our mortal bodies, and your wife and children came out of their grave clad in immortal splendor."

When Andrews returned to Switzerland he became sick with tuberculosis also. He continued working - printing, publishing, preaching but also praising the Lord for his constant blessings. On October 21, 1883, he passed away. A marble stone at the cemetery in Basel, Switzerland, marks his grave. His wife, Angeline, is buried in Rochester, New York, in Mt. Hope Cemetery. Buried on her right is Carrie Matilda Andrews, who died of dysentery when she was just a little more than a year old. Buried on her mother's left is Mary Frances Andrews.

More Interesting Facts

*His father's ancestors landed at Plymouth 18 years after the arrival of the *Mayflower*.

*Andrews University and Andrews Academy in Berrien Springs, Michigan, are named after John Andrews, as well as the primary school in Takoma Park, Maryland.

*J. N. Andrews could read the entire Bible in seven languages, including Latin, Greek, Hebrew and French.

*Andrews admitted that he could quote the entire New Testament from memory, but he was not quite sure about making a word-perfect recital of the Old Testament.

*Andrews was chairman of the founding committee that drew up the constitution of the General Conference.

The Andrews family: John, his wife, Angeline, and children, Charles and Mary.

John Andrews, age 44, leaving Boston harbor with his children heading for Switzerland.

Mary Andrews

Four generations of Andrews missionaries: The son, Charles remained in Switzerland. Later grandson, Dr. John Nevins Andrews, would be the first missionary to Tibet. Many more would follow him.

(Left) John Andrews and Willie White.
(Right) J. N. Andrews' parents, Edward and Sarah Pottle Andrews

(Left) John Andrews' grave in Switzerland.
(Right) A closer view of Andrews' grave in Basel, Switzerland. Andrews requested no eulogy be printed in Adventist publications about him.

(Left) Charles E. Bradford, administrator, pastor and author wrote about the Sabbath in Africa. John Nevins Andrews first introduced research showing that there were faithful seventh-day Sabbath observers in Africa in his volume *The History of the Sabbath and First Day of the Week* in 1859. Ellen White employed his research in her most influential work, *The Great Controversy*. Charles E. Bradford would use these statements to investigate the history and roots of the Sabbath in Africa and write his book *Sabbath Roots: The African Connection*.
(Right) Sabbath Roots, by C. E. Bradford

In 1877 Maude Sisley Boyd joined J. N. Andrews in Switzerland, the first Adventist single female called to foreign service. Maude set type for the first tracts in Italian, learning on the job.

House in Neuchatel where J. N. Andrews first stopped in Switzerland at Albert F. Vuilleumier's, 1874-1875

Legacy of Leadership. An outdoors sculpture by Alan Collins finished in 1998 at Andrews University campus in Berrien Springs, Michigan. It stands in front of the Pioneer Memorial Church.

Second stopping place of Elder Andrews at La Coudre near Neuchatel 1875-1876

First house occupied at Basel, Switzerland, by Elder Andrews where Sister Maud Sisley Boyd set the type for *Les Signes des Temps* and tracts (1876-1882).

5. 7. GEORGE IDE BUTLER
First Term: December 29, 1871-August 10, 1874
Second Term: October 6, 1880-October 17, 1888
(Total of 10 one-year terms)

Age When Elected President: 37 years, 1 month
Second time: 45 years
Secretary: Uriah Smith, S. Brownsberger
Treasurer: Mrs. A. P. Van Horn, E. B. Gaskill, Mrs. M. J. Chapman, A. R. Henry
Church Membership When Elected: 4,801

Born: November 12, 1834, in Waterbury, Vermont
Died: July 25, 1918, in Healdsburg, California. He was 83 years old.

Mother: Sarah Growe Butler
Father: Ezra Pitt Butler II, a starch manufacturer, strong Baptist, and a deacon in his church.
Siblings: He was the 4th of six children; Ann, William, Aurora, George, Mary and Martha (the last two girls, Mary and Martha, were twins).
Wife: March 10, 1859, married Lentha A. Lockwood. She was a paralyzed invalid for the last twelve years of her life. She died in Bowling Green, Florida (1826-1901).
Elizabeth Work Grainger- married 1907
Children: Annie (1861- 1874)
William Pitt-(1864-1948)
Hiland George-(1864-1929). Although he and his brother William were twins, Hiland was killed in an auto accident and died nearly 20 years before his brother.
Baptized: 1856 by J. N. Andrews in Waukon, Iowa
Ordained: 1867 by James White and Augustine C. Bourdeau
Church Affiliation of parents: Baptists
Year family became Adventists: 1843
Buried: White Sandy Cemetery, Bowling Green, Florida, between the graves of his first wife, Lentha, and his sister, Aurora (Aurora married Ransom Lockwood, the brother of George Butler's wife, Lentha Lockwood).

Expansion. Youngest president. Evangelist.

George Ide Butler was born in Waterbury, Vermont, November 12, 1834. His family was well known in Vermont. His grandfather, Ezra Pitt Butler, began life as a farmer, served as a soldier in the Revolutionary War, was a Baptist preacher and later became a politician and governor of Vermont from 1826 to 1828.

George's father, Ezra Pitt Butler II, was a starch manufacturer and a deacon in the Baptist Church. In 1843 the Butler family left the Baptist Church and prepared for Christ's return with other Millerites. When Christ did not return on October 22, 1844, they were greatly disappointed. George, only nine years old, was not able to understand all that had taken place. The jeers and mockery turned him against all religion and he remained a skeptical unbeliever until he was twenty-two years old. In 1848 Ezra Butler accepted the doctrine of the Sabbath from Joseph Bates and was ordained to the ministry in 1853.

George's father had two large starch factories in Stowe, Vermont, when he joined the Adventist Church. He immediately stopped all work on the Sabbath in his starch plants, but he also had to close on Sunday because the workers would not work on Sunday. God blessed him even with his factories closed two days of the week. Elders James White, Evarts and Hart ordained Ezra Butler to the gospel ministry but he never felt that he had the proper training to do much preaching.

Three generations of Butlers had lived in Vermont when James White appealed to the Butlers to move westward to strengthen the work there. Ezra Butler moved his little family to a farm in Waukon, Iowa. Longing for some excitement George left his father and the farm and joined a surveying party. After tramping through the wilderness for a long time he settled down on a homestead in Minnesota for a short while. He then found a job working on a ship that sailed down the Mississippi and Missouri rivers.

For a while his life seemed pointless and without direction until the words of Philippians 4:8 came to his mind "Whatsoever things are true, whatsoever things are honest, whatsoever things are just, whatsoever things are pure, whatsoever things are lovely, whatsoever things are of good report; if there be any virtue, and if there be any praise think on these things." A voice seemed to speak to him saying "Why not believe all the good things in the Bible?" All of a sudden he thought of God and he hurried back to his home and in his small cabin he fell on his knees and surrendered his life to God.

When he returned to his father's farm he discovered that the Andrews family had moved into the neighborhood and he began to study with John Andrews and soon J. N. Andrews baptized George. George taught school for two years and in 1859 he married Lentha Lockwood.

George Butler became a church elder and threw all of his energy into his work. When the leaders of the Iowa Conference needed to be replaced (B. F. Snook and W. H. Brinkerhoff had defected from the faith and had divided the Adventist believers in Iowa), they appointed George Butler in 1865 as the president of the Iowa Conference. In 1867, two years after he became president, he was ordained to the gospel ministry. Even as president he conducted several series of evangelistic meetings. Six years after Butler's ordination he was elected president of the General Conference (while still president of the Iowa Conference). He spent much of his time traveling from New England to California, holding many evangelistic meetings. The camp meetings also flourished, rallying the believers and adding thousands of new members to the church.

At the close of his first period as General Conference president James White's health had improved so White became president and Elder Butler returned to Iowa as conference president. Then he was reelected as General Conference president. During his second period of leadership he traveled to Europe and while there laid the groundwork for a publishing house in England and later two others in Switzerland and in Norway.

Early Adventist preachers were self-supporting and often self-trained. They would work for the church for a while and then return to oversee their farms and crops. In 1883 Butler wrote about the subject of tithing and how it not only blessed the members but would also pay the ministers' salaries so that they could devote their full time to work for the Lord. Tithe was not to be used for church building maintenance and repairs but for the support of the gospel ministry. His emphasis on the correct use of the Bible tithing system was a practice which placed the church on a sound financial basis for the first time.

He wanted a better-trained ministry so, with James and Ellen White, he actively raised funds for Battle Creek College which opened its doors in 1874. He also gave enthusiastic support for the Whites' dream of establishing a new publishing house on the West Coast, resulting in the founding of the Pacific Press.

When he began his second period as president, the church witnessed the greatest percentage growth in the denomination's history. He helped organize evangelistic teams which pitched tents in hundreds of towns, stressing the need to observe the law of God. Although good for church growth, Ellen White would later say that this emphasis had left the church "as dry as the hills of Gilboa." His relentless work kept him from attending the 1888 General Conference session in Minneapolis when Elder Olsen was elected as president.

Butler retired to Florida and purchased 115 acres which he called "Twin Magnolias." His strength returned once he was free of the constant executive pressure, but his wife became paralyzed and for twelve years he faithfully provided nursing care for her until her death. Then at age 67 he accepted the request to become the first president of the Florida Conference and later the first president of the Southern Union. In 1907 he married Mrs. Elizabeth Granger, the widow of Professor W.C. Granger, who had been a missionary to Japan.

More Interesting Facts

*Grandfather Ezra Pitt was a farmer, preacher, soldier and the Governor of Vermont from 1826 to 1828.

*One of Butler's converts in a tent meeting in Iowa was ten-year-old Arthur G. Daniells who would later become the General Conference president.

*Butler was the youngest person to be elected as the world president, being elected at only 37 years of age (37 years and one month). John Andrews was also elected when he was 37 (37 years and 7 months).

*Butler had to deal with one of the brightest stars and successful preachers of the Adventist Church, Dudley Canright. Canright rejected Ellen White as a prophet and left the Adventist Church. Butler blended kindness and firmness in dealing with him.

The Butler's children: Annie and the twin boys, William and Hiland.

ELDER GEORGE IDE BUTLER

(Left) George Butler as General Conference president.
(Right) Elder Butler on the cover of the *Adventist Review* announcing his death.

Ezra Butler II, the father of George Butler. Ezra's father and George's grandfather was Ezra Pitt Butler,
who had been governor of Vermont in 1826.

(Left) Twenty-six year old Charles M. Kinney attended an evangelistic meeting held by J. N. Loughborough in 1878, and became one of the charter members of the church in Reno, Nevada. He heard one sermon by Ellen White. The Reno members sent him to study for two years at Healdsburg College and he did colporteur work for a short time. He was sent to open the work in Kansas and helped start the first black church still in existence today in Louisville, Kentucky. He became the first ordained African American Adventist minister.
(Rght) C. M. Kinney teaching a class (Adele Warren and wife on far left).

Butler Hall, the men's dorm, was built and completed in 1908 on Oakwood College's campus and named after George I. Butler, who had been chairman of Oakwood's board when he was the first president of the Southern Union (after being president of the General Conference).

(Left) Martha Butler. She and her twin sister Mary were the younger siblings of George Butler.
She married William Andrews and went to Switzerland to help her brother-in-law, John.
(Right) William Butler, son of George Butler.

(Left) The grave site of Ezra Pitt Butler.
(Right) Mrs. Lentha Butler, wife of George Butler.

Sessions of the General Conference of Seventh-day Adventists

Sessions	Delegates	Opening Date	Place
1	20	May 20, 1863	Battle Creek, Michigan
2	20	May 18, 1864	Battle Creek, Michigan
3	21	May 17, 1865	Battle Creek, Michigan
4	19	May 16, 1866	Battle Creek, Michigan
5	18	May 14, 1867	Battle Creek, Michigan
6	15	May 12, 1868	Battle Creek, Michigan
7	16	May 18, 1869	Battle Creek, Michigan
8	22	March 15, 1870	Battle Creek, Michigan
9	17	February 7, 1871	Battle Creek, Michigan
10	14	December 29, 1871	Battle Creek, Michigan
11	18	March 11, 1873	Battle Creek, Michigan
12	21	November 14, 1873	Battle Creek, Michigan
13	19	August 10, 1874	Battle Creek, Michigan
14	18	August 15, 1875	Battle Creek, Michigan
1st Special Session	15	March 31, 1876	Battle Creek Michigan
15	16	September 19, 1876	Lansing, Michigan
2nd Special Session	16	November 12, 1876	Battle Creek, Michigan
16	20	September 20, 1877	Lansing, Michigan
3rd Special Session	22	March 1, 1878	Battle Creek Michigan
17	39	October 4, 1878	Battle Creek, Michigan
Special Session	29	April 17, 1879	Battle Creek, Michigan
18	39	November 7, 1879	Battle Creek, Michigan
5th Special Session	28	March 11, 1880	Battle Creek, Michigan
19	38	October 6, 1880	Battle Creek, Michigan
20	41	December 1, 1881	Battle Creek, Michigan
21	47	December 7, 1882	Rome, New York
22	65	November 8, 1883	Battle Creek, Michigan
23	67	October 30, 1884	Battle Creek, Michigan
24	70	November 18, 1885	Battle Creek, Michigan
25	71	November 18, 1886	Battle Creek, Michigan
26	70	November 13, 1887	Oakland, California
27	91	October 17, 1888	Minneapolis, Minnesota
28	109	October 18, 1889	Battle Creek, Michigan

		(The 28th session voted to hold biennial sessions.)	
29	125	March 5-25, 1891	Battle Creek, Michigan
30	130	February 17-Mar 6, 1893	Battle Creek, Michigan
31	150	February 15-Mar 4, 1895	Battle Creek, Michigan
32	140	February 19-Mar 8, 1897	College View, Nebraska
33	149	February 15-Mar 7, 1899	South Lancaster, Mass.
34	268	April 2-23, 1901	Battle Creek, Michigan
35	139	March 27-April 13, 1903	Oakland, California
36	197	May 11-30, 1905	Washington, DC
		(The 36th session voted to hold quadrennial sessions.)	
37	328	May 13-June 6, 1909	Washington, DC
38	372	May 15-June 8, 1913	Washington, DC
39	443	March 29-April 14, 1918	San Francisco, California
40	581	May 11-28, 1922	San Francisco, California
41	577	May 27-June 14, 1926	Milwaukee, Wisconsin
42	577	May 28-June 12, 1930	San Francisco, California
43	671	May 26-June 8, 1936	San Francisco, California
44	619	May 26-June 7, 1941	San Francisco, California
45	828	June 5-15, 1946	Washington, DC
46	943	July 10-22, 1950	San Francisco, California
47	1,109	May 24-June 5, 1954	San Francisco, California
48	1,160	June 19-28, 1958	Cleveland, Ohio
49	1,314	July 26-Aug 4, 1962	San Francisco, California
50	1,495	June 16-25, 1966	Detroit, Michigan
51	1,782	June 11-20, 1970	Atlantic City, New Jersey
		(The 51st session voted to hold quinquennial sessions.)	
52	1,756	July 10-19, 1975	Vienna, Austria
53	1,925	April 16-26, 1980	Dallas, Texas
54	2,044	June 27-July 6, 1985	New Orleans, LA
55	2,239	July 5-14, 1990	Indianapolis, IN
56	2,321	June 29-July 8, 1995	Utrecht, Netherlands
57	1,844	June 29-July 8, 2000	Toronto, Canada
58	1,903	June 29-July 9, 2005	St. Louis, Missouri
59	2,244	June 23-July 3, 2010	Atlanta, Georgia
60	2,571	July 2-July 11, 2015	San Antonio, Texas

8. OLE ANDRES OLSEN
October 17, 1888-February 19, 1897
(8 years)

Age when elected president: 43 years old (In 1889 it was voted that sessions be every two years instead of every year).
Church Membership When Elected: 25,841
Secretary: Dan T. Jones, W. A. Colcord, L. T. Nicola
Treasurer: Harmon Lindsay, W. H. Edwards

Born: July 28, 1845, in Skogen, Norway
Died: January 29, 1915, in Hinsdale, Illinois. He was 69 years old.
Mother: Bertha Olsen
Father: Andrew Olsen (May 2, 1816-July 29, 1908)
Church Affiliation of parents: Lutheran in Norway; Methodists in America
Year family became Adventists: 1858
Siblings: The oldest of 12 children, three of whom died in infancy
Wife: Jennie Gertrude Nelson (1843-March 17, 1920) Melrose, Massachusetts. She was the oldest daughter of 12 children
Children: Alfred Berthier Olsen (b. June 26, 1869)
Mahlon Ellsworth Olsen (b. March 28, 1873)
Clarence Henry Nils Olsen (died January 7, 1889, at eleven years of age)
Baptized: 1858 by Elder Waterman Phelps
Ordained: June 2, 1873
Buried: Ole Olsen and his wife Jenny are buried in Rock Creek Cemetery in Takoma Park, Maryland

Norwegian. Scandinavian evangelist. Global outlook.

Ole Olsen came to America when he was five years old. His father, Andrew Olsen, was dissatisfied with the then rigid Lutheran State Church of Norway. He also felt dissatisfied with what he termed formality and coldness. He enjoyed studying the Bible and for a while neighbors and friends came to his house for mutual study and discussion of the Scriptures.

One evening a friend said, "If we would follow the Scriptures fully, we ought to keep the seventh day, Saturday, and not Sunday. There is no authority in the Bible for obeying Sunday." Even though this friend was not a seventh day observer the point that he made stuck with Andrew Olsen. For months he searched the Scriptures, comparing texts and hunting answers to this question.

In the meantime, in the spring of 1850 the Olsen family set sail for the United States. It was a long journey of thirteen weeks-nine weeks on the ocean, then four weeks in making the journey from New York by steamboat up the Hudson River, then by the Erie Canal to Buffalo, and from there by steamer to Milwaukee, Wisconsin, finishing with an ox-drawn wagon trip 70 miles westward.

The family joined the Methodist Episcopal Church but additional Bible study convinced them to observe the Sabbath. In three years' time a total of eight families started keeping the Sabbath and were called "Seventh Day Methodists."

Mrs. Olsen prayed for the salvation of her children daily. She called each child by name from the oldest to the youngest. One by one they gave their hearts to God and joined the church. When the youngest had been baptized Bertha Olsen said "My mission work is now finished." When Waterman Phelps came to Oakland in April, 1858, to hold a series of evangelistic meetings, he asked the eight Norwegian families to attend. The young people who spoke English translated the sermons in Norwegian for the older ones. Andrew and his family were baptized. Ole Olsen was thirteen when he and his family became members of the Adventist Church. Andrew Olsen would become the father of a band of ministers who gave their lives to the Adventist Church: Ole A. Olsen would become president of the General Conference, E.G. Olsen and M.M. Olsen administrators, and Albert Olsen who was for years a leader in the publishing work. That casual remark made by someone in Norway, started an interest and inquiry in Andrew Olsen's heart that brought great fruitage in the Adventist movement. Andrew Olsen died in 1908 at the age of ninety-two. Ole finished the elementary grades and at age 19 enrolled at Milton College, the Seventh Day Baptist School which was just a few miles south of his home. He studied there for two winters and in 1866 matriculated at Battle Creek College for special studies. He never completed any degrees.

In 1868 Ole Olsen married a neighborhood sweetheart, Jenny Nelson, and settled on a nearby farm. In 1869 the Wisconsin Conference recognized his abilities and gave him a ministerial license and assigned him to work among the Scandinavians. He held his first evangelistic series in 1871. On June 2, 1873, he was ordained to the gospel ministry and one year later, at age 29, he became president of the Wisconsin Conference. Later he became president of the Dakota Conference, Minnesota Conference and Iowa Conference.

Because he was fluent in Norwegian he accepted the call to go to Scandinavia in 1886. He purchased a tent in England and when he arrived in Oslo, Norway, he pitched it on a lot near one of the Lutheran state churches. His brother E.G. Olsen worked with him and at the close they organized a church of twenty-five members. In 1887 the Norwegian Conference was organized and he was chosen as its president. In October, 1888, at the General Conference session at Minneapolis, Minnesota, even though he was still preaching in Norway and was not at the session, he was chosen by the delegates to be the president of the world church. Ellen White suggested Olsen's name for the presidency. She had spent time with him during his visit to Europe from 1885 to 1887 and was favorably impressed with his spirituality and leadership skills.

Olsen inherited the fallout from the church's most serious theological controversy up to that time. The long-time leaders of the denomination had seen rapid growth follow their vigorous stress on obedience to the law of God. They saw the new focus on justification by faith alone as criticism of their work which had been built upon tears, agony and great personal sacrifice. They were reluctant to admit they had been wrong.

Olsen's tranquil, kindly temperament seemed fashioned for such a time. He was a proven evangelist, experienced in difficult pioneer work, so his standing could hardly be questioned by the "old guard." Yet he offered openness toward the younger ministers, since he stood outside the old establishment. The controversy raged throughout his period as president.

Mrs. White frequently visited the Olsen home and on one occasion she presented a book to each of the two Olsen boys. After he was not reelected as church president in 1897 he went as a missionary to South Africa. In 1901 he was asked to head the work in Great Britain. In 1905 he responded to an invitation from Australia and four years later he returned to the United States as secretary of the newly-formed North American Foreign Department with headquarters in Chicago. Under his leadership, Adventists launched their first mission work among non-Christians to the Matabeles of Rhodesia. He had a vision for world-wide expansion of the Adventist Church.

In 1913 he accepted the post of vice president of the North American Division of Seventh-day Adventists which he held while serving as the director of the North American Foreign Department. Ole Olsen and his wife Jenny are buried in Rock Creek Cemetery in Takoma Park, Maryland. Ellen White was displeased with Olsen's dealings with the treasurers A.R. Henry and Harmon Lindsay and felt that he allowed them to become involved in questionable business practices. Ellen White strongly urged him to replace these two men but he did not do so until near the end of 1895. Ellen White wrote to him about his excessive labor in the cause and cautioned him about working himself to exhaustion.

More Interesting Facts

*James and Ellen White were frequent guests at the Olsen home in Green Bay, Wisconsin.

*In the summer of 1887, Mrs. White visited the Olsen family who were living in Christiana (Oslo), Norway. Together they held the first Adventist camp meeting to take place in Europe, where Ellen White was the main speaker. Although quite a number attended the meetings, there were but two family tents-one for Mrs. White and her secretaries, and one for the Olsens.

*At age 19, young Olsen attended Milton College, a Seventh Day Baptist school that William Spicer's parents had helped to found.

*Olsen was the first General Conference president to visit Africa. He made the difficult trip in 1894 to encourage the missionaries who had opened the first mission station (Solusi) among the Matabele people in Rhodesia.

The Olsen family. Four of the boys became ordained ministers. Ole (O. A.) Olsen front row, left; Andrew (A. D.) Olsen, front row, right; Martin (M.M.) Olsen, standing, left; Edward (E.G.) Olsen, standing, center; Albert (A. J.) Olsen, far right who became a publishing leader. From a photo taken in 1879.

(Left) Andrew Olsen, father and patriarch of Ole Olsen and the Olsen clan.
(Right) President of the General Conference, Ole A. Olsen.

(Left) Jennie Olsen, wife of O. A. Olsen.
(Right) Mrs. Jennie Nelson Olsen in later life, wife of O. A. Olsen.

(Left) The Olsen family around 1900.
(Right) The three sons of Jennie and Ole Olsen: Alfred (A.B) Olsen became a physician and married a physician, Mary Poole. Mahlon (M.E.) Olsen became an administrator and educator with a PhD, and little Clarence died at age eleven.

Elder and Mrs. Olsen enjoy the Moss camp meeting in Norway, 1887.

Elder and Mrs. Olsen in their retirement years on the front porch of their house in Maryland.

At the gravesite of Elder Olsen.

Elder Olsen on the platform as Mrs. White delivers a message.

The Olsen home in Swedberg.

Second son Mahlon (M. E.) Olsen and his family: wife, Lydia D. Christensen Olsen, and children, Louise, Alice, Yvonne and Olan.

The Oakland church was recently remodeled.

August 5, 1969, Vol. LXI, No. 30

The oldest Norwegian Adventist Church in the world, in Wisconsin.

(Left) Andrew (A.D.) Olsen. Second son in the family. He passed away at age 39.
(Right) Edward (E.G.) Olsen. Fourth son of the family.

(Left) Martin (M.M.) Olsen. Third son in the family. He did a great deal of evangelism back in his home country of Norway.
(Right) Albert (A.J.) Olsen. Baby son of the family

Dr. Mary Poole Olsen. She married Ole Olsen's son, Dr. Alfred (A.B.) Olsen.

Dr. Alfred (A.B.) Olsen the son of Ole and Jennie Olsen.

The last photograph of Mrs. E. G. White taken at her home. Standing are some of her secretaries and other helpers. Seated to Mrs. White's left is Elder O.A. Olsen and to her right is her son, W. C. White.

Samuel J. Thompson, one of the first sixteen students to enroll at Oakwood College on its opening day, November 16, 1896. Elder O. A. Olsen had been a part of the three-man committee dispatched in 1895 to locate land for a black school in Huntsville.

9. GEORGE ALEXANDER IRWIN
February 19, 1897-April 2, 1901
(4 years; two two-year terms)

Age When Elected President: 52 years old
Church Membership When Elected: 56,436
Secretary: L. A. Hoopes
Treasurer: A. G. Adams

Born: November 17, 1844, near Mt. Vernon, Ohio
Died: May 23, 1913. He was 68 years old.
Mother: Nancy McCracken Irwin
Father: Isaac Irwin; when Nancy died in 1855 he married Priscilla Johnson in 1866.
Siblings: Gilman and Catherine (both died early); Emily, Harriet, Elsey, Ageline
Wife: Nettie (Antenette) Johnson (1849-1919), a teacher and later a women's dean and cook, married September 17, 1867
Children: Charles Walter Irwin, November 4, 1868

Prisoner. African American work. Australia.

George Irwin was born near Mount Vernon, Ohio in 1844, while America was still dealing with the fallout of the Millerite movement. His early childhood was difficult because his mother died when he was nine years old and his father remarried Priscilla Johnson in 1866. George had to live with relatives on a farm. He assisted with farm chores, attended public schools and worked in the nearby town to help with expenses.

When he was about to enter high school in Mount Vernon he accepted the call of his country to enter the Union army and fight against slavery in the Civil War. At age 17 he enlisted in Company I, Twentieth Regiment Ohio Volunteer Infantry. At the end of his three-year term he reenlisted and served until the close of the war. He took part in seventeen battles and engagements and was captured and imprisoned outside of Atlanta for seven months in the notorious Andersonville prison near Macon, Georgia.

Prison life was very difficult. He was crowded together with thousands of other soldiers with barely anything to eat. Someone gave George a copy of the *Saints' Everlasting Rest* written by an English minister named Baxter. This book encouraged him and led to his conversion. Then he was transferred to Richmond, Virginia, to Libby Prison. He was released at age 22 in time to march in the grand review before the president of the United States which was held in Washington, D. C. at the close of the war. He was fortunate to be alive and to have God in his heart.

George then returned to his old home in Ohio, joined the Congregational Church, and then transferred to the Methodist Church. On September 17, 1867, he married Nettie Johnson (1849-1919), a school teacher, and settled on a farm near Mount Vernon, Ohio. Soon they were the parents of their only child, Charles Walter Irwin who was born November 4, 1868. (Professor Irwin, as this child would become known, was an outstanding teacher and administrator, including being the first president of Pacific Union College and the Director of Education of the General Conference Education Department).

He became a Seventh-day Adventist in 1885 through a series of Bible lectures held in a nearby schoolhouse. When he expressed his desire to work for the church he was made a district director and given charge of a few churches in the vicinity of his home in Ohio. Later he served as treasurer of the Ohio Conference and four years after he accepted the truth he was elected president of the Ohio Conference. In 1895 he was appointed Superintendent of the Southern District and leader of the fledgling Adventist work in the Southern United States. It was here that he developed a special interest in helping African Americans join the mainstream of American and Adventist life.

The denomination asked Ole Olsen (GC president), Harmon Lindsay (a former GC Treasurer) and George Irwin (soon-to-be GC president) to select the school site in the South to educate and train black Adventists. They were given a limit of $8000 to spend and were directed to Huntsville, Alabama, and the 360-acre Beasily plantation about five miles northwest of town. At first all they saw were the worn-out barn and the dilapidated buildings. At one time the Beasily estate had been a frequent refuge for Andrew Jackson and had been a beautiful and fertile place but it had been abandoned and neglected. But the more they inspected their intuition told them that there were great possibilities. They saw sixty-five towering oak trees and they decided to call the place Oakwood.

The three men donned their overalls and with several prospective students started work on clearing the underbrush. The Oakwood School, purchased in late 1895, would begin in 1896 and would grow to become Oakwood University. On official opening date, November 16, 1896, sixteen pupils comprised the charter student body (Etta Littlejohn, one of the sixteen, became the mother of Charles E. Bradford and grandmother of Calvin B. Rock, Oakwood's eighth president). A few years later Mrs. White visited the Oakwood school and was very pleased with the property and the work established for black students. One of the residence halls at Oakwood was named, Irwin Hall, after G. A. Irwin.

Elder Irwin also supported the *Morning Star* boat which James Edson White and W. O. Palmer had built to take education and the gospel to the black people of the South. *The Morning Star* sailed down the Mississippi and stopped often while Edson and the colporteurs on the boat sold books and taught the people on the shore who were interested. They also distributed clothes, meal, flour and molasses. When Elders Irwin and I. H. Evans arrived on the boat they were given a grand tour of the *Morning Star*. The two leaders spoke to believers, inspected the movable chapel and participated in its dedication. The two leaders left just before a mob of prejudiced white men planned to attack the *Morning Star*. Irwin saw to it that needed funds were sent to the struggling mission boat.

At the General Conference session held in Lincoln, Nebraska, in March 1897, Elder Irwin was elected president of the General Conference. He visited Australia in 1899 where Mrs. White was living and Avondale College was being started. Upon his return to the United States he gave enthusiastic reports of the growth of the work there. After serving for four years as General Conference president he was called to the presidency of the Australasian Union Conference to replace Arthur G. Daniells.

Somewhat hurt, he was tempted to think his efforts were unappreciated, but in 1905 he was elected vice president of the General Conference for the North American Division and later called to the presidency of the Pacific Union Conference. He was instrumental in purchasing the Loma Linda property and his last official position was that of president of the Board of Directors of the College of Medical Evangelists, at Loma Linda, a position he would hold to the time of his death.

Mrs. Irwin first became acquainted with Ellen White when Mrs. White wrote them a series of letters from 1890. The Irwins frequently counseled with Ellen White. Nettie was active in the Women's Christian Temperance Union, heading up the department in 1900 after the death of Mrs. S. M. I. Henry. After George's death in 1913, Nettie served as women's dean and later as cafeteria director of the Loma Linda sanitarium.

More Interesting Facts

*In 1907 Irwin wrote *The Spirit of Prophecy: Its Relation to the Law of God and its Place in the Plan of Salvation*.

*A newspaper clipping says Irwin enlisted in the army as a private at age 17 and left as a colonel.

*George Irwin was the first G. C. president to visit Australia.

*In 1910 George Irwin served as president of the Pacific Union Conference while his son, Charles Irwin, served as president of Pacific Union College.

As a young man, Irwin served in the Civil War on the Union side and was captured and suffered greatly in several prisons. This picture from the *Guide* magazine captures that period of his life.

George Alexander Irwin as president of the General Conference.

G. A. Irwin sits on front porch with his wife.

Irwin Hall at Oakwood College in the 1920s built to honor Elder G. A.
Irwin and his part in finalizing on the school's location.

(Left) Professor Charles W. Irwin, son of the president. He was president of Pacific Union College and later Director of the
Department of Education at the General Conference.
(Right) Irwin Hall at Pacific Union College is named for the Irwin family.

Elder A. G. Daniells, the General Conference president, visited the Walla Walla campus in 1907 with former General Conference president G. A. Irwin. They were guided around campus by business manager C. M. Christiansen. The driver of the carriage, a student, is Ross C. Patterson, grandfather of Gary Patterson. Ross later married another student, Kate Schoepflin. Ross and Kate's three children, Glenn, Ella, and June attended Walla Walla College, as well as did several grandchildren and great-grandchildren.

A close-up of the same photo.

George Irwin in his visit to France.

The star of the *Morning Star* which ended up at Oakwood College. Elder Irwin was part of the three man team that was sent
in 1895 to find land for a school for the colored people that had become Adventists as a result of the
Morning Star's evangelistic efforts.

A replica of the *Morning Star* boat that began evangelization for the colored people in the South. Irwin was the district leader in the South that further guided the development of the black work.

ADVENTIST PATRIARCH DIES AT CONFERENCE

Washington, May 23.—Today's session of the Seventh-day Adventists world conference at Takoma Park, Md., came to an abrupt end upon the announcement of the death of Elder G. A. Irwin of Loma Linda, Cal., one of the patriarchs of the denomination and an ex-president of the general conference. Elder Irwin, who died suddenly today of heart failure, was born near Mount Vernon, O., in 1841. He served through the civil war, becoming a colonel in the federal army.

A newspaper clipping in the *Salt Lake Herald* that announces the death of Elder Irwin.

10. ARTHUR GROSVENOR DANIELLS
April 2, 1901-May 11, 1922
(21 years)

Age When Elected President: 42 years old
Church Membership When Elected: 78,188
Secretary: H. E. Osborne, W. A. Spicer
Treasurer: H. M. Mitchell, I.H. Evans, W.T. Knox

Born: September 28, 1858, in West Union, Iowa
Died: March 22, 1935, at Glendale, California. He was 76 years old.
Baptized: George I. Butler baptized Arthur at age 10 in 1868 in Iowa.
Mother: Mary Jane McQuillain-Daniells Lippincott
Father: Dr. Thomas Grosvenor Daniells-Union Army physician and surgeon in the Civil War. Died at age 58 as an officer of the Union Army in the Battle of Antietam in 1863 leaving Arthur fatherless at age five.
Siblings: Besides Arthur who was the eldest son, there were twins, born two years later, Charles and Jessie.
Wife: Married Mary Ellen Hoyt, a childhood friend also of West Union, Iowa, on November 28, 1876, which was Thanksgiving Day and Mary's 22nd birthday.
Children: Dr. Arthur Grosvenor Daniells, Jr., Marylyn Lee Daniells
Ordained: 1882, Iowa
Education: One year at Battle Creek College
Church Affiliation of parents: Methodist
Buried: Forest Lawn Memorial Park Cemetery, Glendale, California

Longest presidency. World War I. GC Secretary, too.

Arthur Grosvenor Daniells was born in West Union, Iowa, September 28, 1858. His father was a medical doctor and served as an officer in the Union Army during the Civil War. He had graduated from the University of Vermont. Dr. Grosvenor drilled a core of older men from Iowa (called the Graybeard Regiment) in military tactics. They found themselves in one of the bloodiest battles of the war at Antietam. Dr. Daniells died from his wounds the next year leaving his family with no means of support and Arthur fatherless at the age of five.

Mrs. Daniells was forced to place her three children in the Veterans' Home, for the children of soldiers. Arthur remained there for about two years until Mrs. Daniels married a West Union rancher by the name of Lippincott. She borrowed a book from a neighbor, *History of the Sabbath* by J.N. Andrews, and after reading it was baptized into the Seventh-day Adventist Church. Arthur worked hard on his step-father's farm and usually had his chores finished before he walked to the one-room country school.

In spite of an impediment in his speech, he finished the local high school and earned sufficient funds working on a neighbor's farm during the summer to pay his way through college for a year. He also received eighty dollars from a pension which the government awarded to the children of soldiers who had given their lives in the Civil War. In the fall of 1875 he left Iowa with seven other young people for Battle Creek College. On November 30, 1876, he married a childhood friend, Mary Ellen Hoyt and he and Mary Ellen taught in nearby country schools.

After one year of teaching, the call to the gospel ministry began to tug at his heart. At first he repelled it, reasoning that he was too timid, too unlearned, and too hesitant. Mary kept urging him to pray more and one day he found a large haystack in the field and crept into a little opening that had been carved out by the cattle.

Here he poured out his soul to God and felt the clear and forceful conviction that he should go and work in God's vineyard.

When he offered his services to the denomination, the Iowa Conference committee rejected him. The next year he joined Robert M. Kilgore in Texas and then became secretary to James and Ellen White for nearly a year. This was the beginning of a close friendship with Ellen White and her son William C. White that would last for the rest of her life. Elder George Butler invited Daniells in 1880 to preach back in Iowa. He was ordained there and began city mission evangelism which consisted of training ten young women to learn the sacred art of explaining the word of God to small groups of people (Bible workers).

In 1886 he received a commission to proceed to New Zealand as a pioneer missionary. He and his wife remained in this area for fourteen years. In 1897 the Australasian Union Conference was organized which included all the church organizations in Australia, New Zealand, Fiji, and other South Sea Islands. He was elected its first president, holding this office until he returned to America. Following instructions from Ellen G. White he was instrumental in moving the headquarters of the Adventist Church to Washington, D.C. The General Conference offices were established in Takoma Park and the Review and Herald built a new building. A sanitarium and college soon arose on the banks of Sligo Creek.

In 1922, at a session of the General Conference held in San Francisco, Elder Daniells' long tenure of office drew to its close. He was then elected secretary of the General Conference and held this office for four years. He had a burden to spiritualize the ministry and formed the Ministerial Association and the *Ministry* magazine.

His close association with Ellen White was a learning experience for him. He was willing to accept her as a very spiritual person but sometimes he had difficulty believing in her as a prophetess. Toward the end of his life he was completely convinced of her role as a prophet and he spent the rest of his life supporting her work and writings. His book *Christ Our Righteousness* is considered by many as being his best. The final revisions of his last book, *The Abiding Gift of Prophecy*, he completed in the hospital the day before his death.

In her last will and testament Ellen White named Daniells as one of the five original trustees of her estate. He was chair of the Ellen G. White Estate from 1915 to 1935. Daniells had a great burden for the education of the Australian ministry. He felt that students shouldn't have to go to America for training since it was so expensive. There was no money available in Australia to build or buy a school so they rented two houses in Melbourne, Australia, and a school opened there on August 24, 1892. It ran for a term of sixteen weeks with about thirty students, ranging in age from 15 to 50 years old.

In time the committee located 1500 acres about 75 miles north of Sydney. The land appeared so poor and sandy that the Australian assistant secretary of agriculture advised it would be a poor investment even at three dollars an acre. Ellen White thought differently. She saw flourishing cultivated land and the school filled with promising students. God blessed the land and school which was soon named Avondale College.

More Interesting Facts

*In 1905, to try to save expenses, it was voted to have the General Conference sessions every four years.

*Daniells was the first evangelist to New Zealand.

*Daniells wrote *The Worldwide Progress of the Advent Message*, *The World War, A World in Perplexity, Christ Our Righteousness*, and *The Abiding Gift of Prophecy*.

*A. G. Daniells' father was a medical doctor and served in the armed forces and his son was a medical doctor and served in the armed forces.

*Mrs. White had been urging Daniells to evangelize the cities but he was slow to move in this direction. When he visited California to see Mrs. White she flatly refused to see him until he should personally lead out in the work of evangelism in the cities in a manner that would inspire complete denominational commitment.

A.G. Daniells as a young man and later as a mature man.

Mrs. Lippencott by second marriage mother of Elder A. G. Daniells.

Daniells' mother, Mrs. Mary Jane McQuillain-Daniells

(Left) Wife of Elder Daniells, Mary Ellen Hoyt Daniells.
(Right) The Daniells family.

Thanksgiving dinner with the James and Ellen White family. Elder A. G. Daniells stands at the head of the table filled with food and the White children and grandchildren, except for the Jaques family, who were not there. The photo was taken between 1930 and 1934.

Jessie Daniells, sister A.G. Daniells.

(Left) Mrs. Daniells in a rickshaw in China.
(Right) Jessie Daniells (Hare), sister of Arthur.

(Left) A.G. Daniells' funeral at Paulson Memorial Hall, Los Angeles, California. Elder Daniells is being borne down the steps of Paulson Hall between two lanes of honorary pallbearers, preceded by the officiating ministers, Elder Watson and Dr. Magan, and Elders Howell and Calkins, Roberts and Froom. The active pallbearers were Elder MacGuire and Dr. Thomason, Dr. Clark and Elder Hackman, Dr. Wirth and Professor Graf.

(Right) Dr. James H. Howard, the uncle of Dr. Eva B. Dykes, was brought into the church through Georgia Harper Spicer when she did Bible work in Washington, D. C. Dr. Howard was a physician and also clerk for the United States government. He took in Eva Dykes and her family when they were abandoned by their father. Dr. Howard sat on many General Conference committees and was instrumental in starting a girl's school in Africa. Dr. Howard wrote several letters to Elder Daniells about the race question.

(Left) A newspaper article announcing that Elder Daniells had been elected again.
He served longer than any other president, twenty-one years.
(Right) A. G. Daniells Jr at his graduation from Washington Missionary College in 1918

Ground breaking for Daniells Hall (men's dormitory) at Loma Linda University, 1941. Photo: Loma Linda Archives.

(Left) A. G. Daniells with a group of young men.
(Right) Mrs. A. G. Daniells and Mrs. W. T. Knox in Chinese apparel

W. H. GREEN
Secretary of the North American Negro Department.

In 1901, the same year that Elder Daniells became president, W. H. Green became an Adventist. Green practiced law in Charlotte and Elizabeth City, North Carolina and in Washington, D. C. He had argued several cases before the United States Supreme Court. He acquired further study and pastored in Pittsburgh, Pennsylvania, Atlanta, Georgia and Washington, D.C. From 1918 to 1928 he was the first secretary of the North American Negro Department of the General Conference.

Daniells, third from left, at Stanborough Park, Britain.

Seated next to each other, Daniells, Spicer, Irwin, at a group picture.

11. WILLIAM AMBROSE SPICER
May 11, 1922—May 28, 1930
(8 years)

Age When Elected President: 56 years old
Church Membership When Elected: 208,771
Secretary: A. G. Daniells, C. K. Meyers
Treasurer: J. L. Shaw

Born: December 19, 1865, in Freeborn, Minnesota
Died: October 17, 1952, in Takoma Park, Maryland. He was 86 years old.
Baptized: 1875, when he was 10 years old.
Mother: Susana Manette Coon (1827-1914), a math and language teacher
Father: Ambrose Coates Spicer (1820-1903), a preacher, carpenter, teacher, administrator, farmer
Siblings: Hale Julian Spicer
      Ettie Manette Spicer
      William Ambrose was the youngest of the three surviving children (two others died in infancy).
Wife: Georgia Eleanora Harper. Married in London, April, 1890.
Children: William Jr; Dorothy; Helen (born in India)
Ordained: Shown as an ordained minister in SDA Yearbook for first time in 1894.
Church Affiliation of parents: Seventh Day Baptist; Seventh-day Adventist
Year family became Adventists; 1874, when William was 9 years old
Buried: Funeral services held at Sligo church in Takoma Park, Maryland, internment at Washington Memorial Cemetery close by.

Secretary. Author. Mission-focused.

Ambrose Coates Spicer graduated from Alfred University, a Seventh Day Baptist school and studied further at Oberlin and Union College in Schenectady, New York. He married Susana M. Coon who had graduated with distinction from the DeRuyters Institute and was one of the few women of her time with a Master's Degree and certified to teach mathematics and languages. She was also accomplished in drawing and painting and came from a long line of Seventh Day Baptists.

After their marriage, they taught at Alfred University and then they were sent by the Seventh Day Baptists from New York to help found and teach in Milton Academy in Wisconsin which later became a college. From the opening of the fall term in 1851, A.C. Spicer had supervision of the Academy for most of seven years, with the assistance of his wife, Mrs. Susana M. Spicer. Their compensation was derived entirely from tuition fees. Later, when they moved to Minnesota, William Ambrose Spicer was born in a log cabin on December 19, 1865.

One of Mr. Spicer's ministerial friends, D.S. Curtiss, became a Seventh-day Adventist. Perturbed by this, Mr. Spicer visited him to persuade him to leave the strange denomination. Mr. Spicer failed completely and instead Mr. Curtis convinced him that the strange denomination was the true biblical church. The family then heard the message more fully at a tent meeting and Mr. and Mrs. Spicer joined the Adventist Church in 1874 when William was nine years old. At the Winona, Minnesota, camp meeting, it was voted to issue him credentials. Mr. Spicer's health was not very good so he turned to farming to recuperate.

As a child William Spicer walked two miles to his elementary schoolhouse. In the spring, while his father plowed, the children followed down the furrows, and William jumped over the snakes that the plow turned out of the rich black soil. There were cows, horses, and sheep to be cared for, and in the summer wild berries to be picked.

The Spicer family moved from Minnesota to Battle Creek the next year and Mr. Spicer became a cabinetmaker while his wife taught French and German at the newly organized Battle Creek College. Here in Battle Creek young William was baptized at age ten in 1875.

William had to quit school when his father suffered a mild stroke and William became a messenger boy, elevator boy, bookkeeper and finally a stenographer at the Sanitarium. He used his evenings to teach himself typing and shorthand, then became a personal secretary to Dr. John Harvey Kellogg. Perhaps the most important thing William did that summer was to read the book *The Great Controversy* which led to his decision to devote his life to the ministry rather than to remain an institutional worker.

In 1885 William met Georgia Eleanora Harper, who had become a schoolteacher in her teens. They became very good friends when she came to Battle Creek to study nursing. Georgia was from Michigan where her father, a doctor, had died when she was just five years old. Georgia later went to Washington, D. C. as a Bible worker. One of her converts was Dr. James Howard, the uncle and supporter of Dr. Eva B. Dykes, the first black lady to receive a PhD. Degree. In the meantime William Spicer, now twenty-two years old, accepted an offer to become a secretary to Stephen N. Haskell who was in charge of foreign missions for the General Conference. At that time there were few stenographers in the conference offices and General Conference men often took a stenographer or secretary with them as they traveled in the field.

When Haskell went to England William Spicer went with him and lived in London. Later he was promoted to editorial work and worked on *Present Truth* as an apprentice to the editor, E.J. Waggoner. William saved enough money from his small salary to pay for Georgia's boat fare across the ocean and they were married in England in April, 1890.

At the end of 1891 he was called back to Battle Creek as secretary of the Foreign Mission Board. In 1894 they returned to London, where Elder Spicer took up editorial work once more. In 1898 he was sent to India as editor of the *Oriental Watchman* and to do ministerial work. At one time he was the only ordained Seventh-day Adventist minister on the whole continent of Asia. He was a delegate to the General Conference of 1901 and was elected secretary of the Mission Board again.

While in India they saw so many neglected children sleeping in the streets that they began gathering them in until they didn't have room for them. Finally, they bought a farm and an orphanage which Mrs. Spicer helped to run. Mrs. Spicer had learned Hindustani and Elder Spicer, Bengali. Mrs. Spicer contracted amoebic dysentery in India and suffered from it as an invalid until she passed away.

In 1903 Elder Spicer became secretary of the General Conference, a position he held until elected president in 1922. In his positions in the General Conference he had to be gone for many long periods of time, once up to eleven months. He calculated that he had been away from home nearly 40 years of his married life. As his heart was touched he would pledge money for the work, money that they really didn't have since he was caring for his mother, sister, and brother as well as Georgia. He would always say that God would provide.

Elder Spicer never owned a car because he never had money to buy one. He was self-educated. Whenever he could get away he spent days at the Library of Congress in Washington. Sometimes he would forget to eat. He also learned German well enough to preach in that language. During World War I Elder Spicer went to Germany from England leaving his Bible and other possessions behind so he could carry some supplies to the workers there.

He made it almost a religion to learn the names of all the workers. He would personally write to each one, visit them in their fields of service, even at the remotest stations, and share their problems. He knew their children by name. Not only did he know the names of the workers at home and abroad but he could also recall when and where he met them, how they looked, or what they said at that time. When riding the train Spicer never paid extra to sleep in a Pullman car except for the few times that Georgia accompanied him.

After he had served eight years as General Conference president he became a general field secretary at age 65. He held that post for ten more years, during which time he also served for a while as associate editor or editor of the *Review.* Although he wrote many books, he never accepted the royalties from these books but put that money back into the work.

Elder Spicer always carried a stub of a pencil in his right coat pocket, along with sheets of paper. He constantly jotted down faults, anecdotes, and mission experiences for his sermons. All of his writing was in pencil. Large calluses developed on the two fingers of his right hand that held this pencil.

Georgia Spicer died on August 5, 1960, in Silver Spring, Maryland. Spicer College near Poona, India, stands as a memorial to him. For fifty years Elder Spicer made regular contributions to the *Review and Herald,* most of the time as an associate editor, but for a brief period as editor.

More Interesting Facts

*Susana Manette Coon and Hannah Coon were sisters. Hannah Coon was the mother of Ella Eaton Kellogg, the wife of Dr. John Harvey Kellogg. Susana Coon was Elder Spicer's mother. So Ella Kellogg (and by marriage, Dr. Kellogg) and William Spicer were first cousins.

*Spicer wrote many books. His most notable are *Our Day in the Light of Prophecy, Miracles of Modern Missions, The Hand That Intervenes, Pioneer Days, The Spirit of Prophecy in the Remnant Church* and *Certainties of the Advent Movement.*

*W. A. Spicer's father grew up as a Baptist. As he studied the Bible alone, he was impressed that the seventh day was the Sabbath and expressed his desire to keep it. A wealthy Baptist offered to send him to a Baptist University for a six-year course, all expenses paid if he would forget about the Sabbath. Spicer turned the offer down to go to Alfred University to keep the Sabbath (as a Seventh Day Baptist). He would later become a Seventh-day Adventist.

(Left) William Ambrose Spicer
(Right) W. A. Spicer's father, Ambrose C. Spicer

Milton College in 1873 started by W. A. Spicer's mother and father.

(Left) W. A. Spicer's sister, Etta Spicer
(Right) William and Etta Spicer

(Left) W. A. Spicer's mother, Susana Coon Spicer
(Right) W. A. Spicer's brother, Hale Julian Spicer

The Spicer children, William Jr., Dorothy, and Helen (born in India)

The Spicer family

London Mission Workers. W. A. Spicer, back row, second from left with his pencil. Georgia Spicer, front row, second from left. Photo: Center for Adventist Research.

William and wife, Georgia

 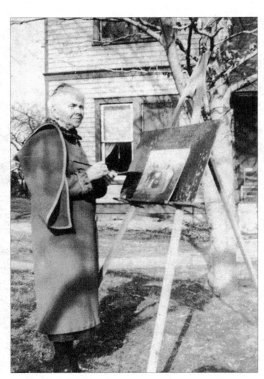

(Left) Etta Spicer painting at her home in Takoma Park, Maryland
(Right) An older Etta still painting. She taught at Columbia Union College.

Ella Kellogg (Mrs. John Harvey Kellogg). Ella Kellogg's mother was a sister to Susana Spicer

Spicer Memorial College, named after W. A. Spicer, has now been elevated to a university.

Spicer Memorial College at its 100th anniversary

Walla Walla College 1904 Graduating class. 1st Row: Irene Kelly (Normal), Pastor W. A. Spicer
(General Conference Secretary), Charles C. Lewis, (President WWC 1902- 1904), Guy F. Wolfkill, Lydia Kime
(Class Secretary). Back Row: Eva Kinney, Gertrude Giles, William George Casebeer, Jessie Aaron Miller,
Harold Kinney, Vina Traver or Verna Travis, Eva Niels, Viola Spence.

Dr. Eva Beatrice Dykes, the first black American woman to complete the requirements for a PhD degree June 21, 1921.
She received her degree from Radcliffe University, an exclusive Ivy-League college for women. Her uncle, Dr. James H.
Howard, was brought into the church through Georgia Harper Spicer when she did Bible work in Washington, D. C.

A montage of photos from the life of William A. Spicer.

W. A. Spicer, front center, with the first Indians to be ordained to the gospel ministry, while he lived in India from 1898 to 1901. Photo: Adventist Review Online, January 28, 2015.

12. CHARLES HENRY WATSON
May 28, 1930-May 26, 1936
(6 years)

Age When Elected President: 52 years old
Church Membership When Elected: 314,253
Secretary: C. K. Meyers, M. E. Kern
Treasurer: J. L. Shaw

Born: Aringa, Victoria, Australia, on October 8, 1877
Died: December 24, 1962, in the Sydney Sanitarium and Hospital. He was 85 years old.
Father: Henry Greaves Watson, wool sorter and trader/buyer, store owner
Mother: Sarah Jane Pettingill. Mrs. Watson couldn't write, but was very practical and ran the family farm and store.
Siblings: 11 brothers and sisters
Married: March 23, 1898, to Elizabeth Mary Shanks (nicknamed "Min") (December 8, 1875-May 16, 1963)
Baptized: In Yambuk Lake, 1902
Education: 1907-1909 attended Australasian Missionary College (Avondale College); returned to Avondale to study under Robert Hare whom he admired
Children: Beatrice, Phyllis, Wilfred, Cyril
Ordained: September 14, 1912, at age 35
Buried: Northern Suburbs Cemetery, Sydney, Australia

Financial acumen. Australian. Great Depression.

The ninth man to be elected president was the only Australian to hold the office. Charles Watson's parents had operated a farm and store and his father had been in the wool buyers' business. It is said that Australia had more sheep than people. Mrs. Watson, called Granny Watson by her twelve children and the neighbors, couldn't read but was tough and practical. Her speech was mixed with the neighboring aborigine language and she couldn't write. But Granny Watson gave her family a practical education in planting, sowing, working in the family store and surviving on the tough Australian farm. Young Charles Watson later owned the business for a short time and had learned to buy and sell wool at a profit. He became a successful businessman in Australia.

The Watson family belonged to the Church of England and were quite religious. When some of his family became Adventists, they bitterly opposed their new faith. While attending the funeral of his sister Adeline, Charles met Pastor W. A. Hennig and was so impressed by him and his funeral sermon that his opposition turned to interest. Mr. and Mrs. Watson asked Pastor Hennig to stay with them after the funeral and explain the Adventist doctrines to the non-Adventist members of the family. They accepted the Adventist message but Charles was not convinced yet. Charles read the book *Bible Readings for the Home Circle* and to his surprise found no biblical support for Sunday as a day of worship.

A neighbor girl, Elizabeth Mary Shanks (Charles called her Min), when she was only two years old, had asked if she could hold the newborn baby Charles on her knees. Charles and Elizabeth grew up together and attended the same schools, church and social functions. They would marry some twenty years later when he was twenty-one and be baptized together when he was converted to Adventism in 1902 at the age of 25.

When Charles and his wife became Adventists he left his business and went to Avondale College to study for the ministry and graduated in 1909. After a short time in the field Charles learned that Pastor Robert Hare, one of his mentors and father of the master storyteller Eric B. Hare, had accepted the post of Bible teacher at Avondale, so he returned to the school for two more years of Bible study under Hare's special tutelage. Some people say that Watson picked up many of the mannerisms, voice inflections and gestures of his teacher Pastor Hare. At any rate, Charles Watson became an outstanding preacher and evangelist.

Six years after his graduation from Avondale, the Australasian Union Conference made Watson its president and he spent a great deal of his planning and preaching among the nomadic Australian aborigines and South Sea islanders. He wrote a book telling of the progress in this area called *Cannibals and Head-Hunters, Victories of the Gospel in the South Seas* (1926).

Watson believed in the foreign mission program of the church. He believed in sending missionaries overseas but he felt that the missionaries should train the nationals so that they could take over their jobs. He felt that the task of the expatriate was to work themselves out of their jobs as soon as possible. In Japan, in the South Pacific, in Africa, all over the world, he pushed for a strong mission program.

In 1918 Watson made his first trip to the United States at the age of forty to attend the General Conference session in San Francisco. When he returned to Australia, with only one year of experience to his credit as a conference president, he was elected vice president of the Australasian Union (Division) and two years later as its president. He reorganized and invigorated the health food industry and turned it into one of the most profitable business ventures in the country. Before this time, it had been handled as a department of the church. Four years later he was made a General Conference vice-president and at the same time an associate treasurer of the General Conference. Four years later a cancer was removed from his bowel. He returned home to Australia expecting to die. Instead, he made a miraculous and complete recovery and lived another forty-one years.

In 1930 the world entered the Great Depression years, and during the next six years Watson's election to and leadership of the General Conference was blessed of God. Early 1932 found him travelling in Europe fighting the fires of disruption and discord ignited by the departure of influential leader Louis Conradi. He returned to Washington in early March weary and distressed only to find he faced more demoralizing dissent and discord nearer to home.

Although he never saw her, Ellen G. White made a tremendous influence on Watson. He maintained a file of quotations from her writings which he richly added to all of his sermons. He believed in the principles that she espoused especially the ones about shunning debt and keeping our institutions free from debt.

The global financial crisis had intensified and Watson was faced with the need to immediately cut appropriations by twelve per cent for the remainder of the year. Just where to apply the cuts he did not know but General Conference salaries was one place to start. The decision was announced with the explanation that headquarters was simply unable to fund its current level of operation. Other strategies involved reducing the general level of administrative expense across the wider church. Achieving efficiency, doing more with less, was the order of the day.

One story from Australia (see *Record*, June 18, 1988, "Who Am I?" by Alan Smith) relates how Pastor Watson himself, just before the banks closed during the Great Depression, tried all day to convince a General Conference committee that it should withdraw its funds from their bank. Eventually the committee agreed and Pastor Watson went to the bank after closing hours. He walked straight in, even though tellers thought they had locked the doors. Once inside the bank he was met with an incredulous bank manager who demanded to know how he had got through a door that he, the manager, had just locked. Now inside the bank, Pastor Watson telegraphed sufficient appropriations to each of the world divisions to keep them operating until the banks opened again. Watson's withdrawal of Adventist funds was the last withdrawal made at that bank. The next day the bank was locked and remained so for several weeks by decree of the president of the United States.

Another story which had been published four time in the *Review* was quite well researched to substantiate the facts (See *Review*, "A Story Revisited," February, 2005, by Merle Poirier) and is probably the correct one. The story takes place in March, 1933, when W. H. Williams, undertreasurer of the General Conference, is impressed to take a trip to New York City to do some unscheduled banking transactions. Prior to this trip, he has been directing his secretary to place units of $1,000 in envelopes (ten one hundred dollar bills) that have been withdrawn monthly from the General Conference bank account into an office safe with no further explanation as to why the cash is being kept outside of the normal banking practices. Williams leaves Thursday, March 2, on the midnight train from Union Station in Washington, D. C. and arrives in New York City early Friday morning. When the banks open for business, Williams proceeds to two different banks that hold accounts for the General Conference and makes two separate transactions that involve sending funds for three months in advance to most of the overseas missions.

Williams returns to his home just before sunset and rejoices in the Lord's care and providence as he keeps the Sabbath. When the sun sets, he is summoned to the GC for an urgent meeting and finds the officers distraught over the news that the banks are closed and wondering where funds will come from to allow them to keep the missionaries in the field and pay salaries since no one knew when the banks would open again.

The meeting turns from a session of despair into a meeting of praise when Williams tells them about his response to a strong impression to go to New York and send funds the previous day and shows them the envelopes in the GC safe in $1,000 increments which are just enough to meet the employee payroll.

Whether Watson did the transactions or Williams, Watson gave God praise at the General Conference Session in 1936 (June 18, p. 296) in the *Review*. "It will be recalled that in this country at one time every bank was closed by Presidential decree. Had I the time tonight to tell you the marvelous and providential ways in which we were led it would thrill your hearts, but let me say simply, without giving you the details, that entirely without any human wisdom or sacrifice and merely upon the impressions that were made upon our hearts by the Spirit of the Lord, the General Conference, when that moment of crisis and bank closure was reached, was financial prepared for it. We were led in that preparation definitely by the Spirit of God."

It is said that Pastor Watson had a photographic memory and a quick analytical mind. He could look over a financial statement and in a few minutes analyze the health of an institution. He had a remarkable ability to remember names and faces. Under his leadership a number of conferences merged and the total workforce was reduced significantly, especially in North America. The painful process helped renew the spirituality of the church and more than 90,000 new members joined the denomination and more than 1000 new church buildings were erected. Watson's refusal to borrow funds proved to be a wise way of operating. In 1932 plans for a theological seminary were put in place and the *Church Manual* was issued.

When Watson and a number of Adventists left Sydney coming to the General Conference session in San Francisco in 1930 aboard the *R. M. S. Niagara* they all traveled third class. Someone asked why they were traveling third class and he replied "Because there is no fourth class." When they were invited to an early tea in the third class dining room and endeavored to make a selection from the sparse vegetarian dishes one of the Adventists commented that there is an old saying that plain living and high thinking go together. "After that meal my thoughts should hit the stars," replied Watson. When the third class chef learned that they were vegetarians he turned out a variety of the finest vegetarian dishes one could wish for, for the rest of the journey and the Adventist party became the envy of the other passengers.

His many travels coupled with his long hours of work, counselling and meetings took its toll on Watson. His health suffered first, and after just one six year term of service he decided to leave the responsibilities of president of the world church and return to Australia. In later life, all four of Watson's children who felt neglected by his devotion to his responsibilities, became disaffected with the church and left. Preacher's kids (PKs) sometimes struggle with the fact that Dad is always gone and is always helping other people and neglecting his own family.

On Thursday, September 17, 1953, little Carolyn Elizabeth Watson, who would have been eight had she lived until September 21, passed away quietly to her rest in the home of her parents, Brother and Sister Cyril Watson (Elder Watson's youngest son). Stricken down by a painful illness, this brave little girl endured much pain until the end.

Just as a funeral was the beginning of the Watson family relationship with the Adventist Church, a funeral caused a new relationship with the Church for Carolyn's father, Cyril Watson. Elders L. C. Naden and J. Trim conducted the service which pointed the sorrowing parents and loved ones present to the glad reunion day soon to come. Pastor Trim (father of David Trim, Director of the Office of Statistics and Archives) affirmed that Cyril was once again reconciled to the church. The family later printed an announcement in the church paper, the *Record*, expressing their thanks and sincere appreciation for all the kind messages of love and sympathy expressed to them. They particularly wanted to thank the Voice of Prophecy staff for their prayers on little Carolyn's behalf. Cyril and his wife, Ada, remained faithful to the church until they passed away many years later.

After his term at the General Conference Elder Watson returned to his homeland, and after a short rest, became the president of the Australasian Division again and a Vice President of the General Conference. His books, *The Atoning Work of Christ* (1934) and The *Promise of the Father* (1936) were published during this time and showed that he was also a great theologian. He retired in 1944 in Turramurra, Australia. He passed away quietly in 1962 and five months later his beloved Min followed him.

Charles Henry Watson will always be remembered as a man of financial integrity, a supporter of overseas missions, a theologian and a man of excellent business acumen.

More Interesting Facts

*Because of the Great Depression and the great expense of having a General Conference session, the normal quadrennial session term of service was extended temporarily from four years to six years. Thus Watson served the longest single term ever–six years.

*The South Queensland Conference has honored the memory of this outstanding leader by naming its convention center Watson Park and the boy's dorm at Avondale College is named Watson Hall.

*Watson suffered from arthritis and other stress-related health problems.

*During his retirement Watson enjoyed gardening and grew prize roses.

*Watson was the first president without a beard. All presidents after him came to the office without the famous beard.

*Watson was the first president not to know Mrs. White personally. He, along with all presidents after him, relied on Mrs. White's writings for guidance.

Charles H. Watson, the only president from Australia.

The Watson Children at the Wahroonga Church School in 1917.
Phyllis, standing second from left; seated on second row; Cyril and Wilfred 4th and 6th from left.

Adventist pioneer leaders with their gorgeous beards. Watson wore no beard and all presidents after him were clean-shaven.

Dr. Horace Shaw of Andrews University looking at Watson's trunk which held his books.

Watson at a ministerial meeting around 1940 in Britain. Elder Watson is standing behind the two men seated on the left.

Watson and South Pacific believers

Watson welcoming his successor, James McElhany

13. JAMES LAMAR McELHANY, Jr.
May 26, 1936-July 10, 1950
(14 years)

Age When Elected President: 56 years old
Church Membership When Elected: 438,139
Secretary: E. D. Dick
Treasurer: W. E. Nelson

Born: January 3, 1880, in Santa Maria, California
Died: June 25, 1959, in Glendale, California. He was 79 years old.
Mother: Mary Ford McElhany
Father: James Lamar McElhany Sr., a self-taught preacher for the Christian Church who later became an Adventist
Siblings: Marcus, Roy, Warren, and three other brothers and sisters
Baptized: October, 1895, at the age of 15, by Pastor S. Thurston
Wife: August 3, 1902, Cora Belle Ackerman at Santa Barbara, California, a nurse (She died August 12, 1939)
　　　July 22, 1942, Matilda Krieger, Glendale, California
Children: Esther (Mrs. John D. Knox), Ruth
Ordained: 1904 by G. A. Irwin, E. W. Farnsworth, S. M. Cobb and G. B Starr in Australia.
Education: Healdsburg College
Buried: Forest Lawn Memorial Park Cemetery, Glendale, California, not far from the grave site of Arthur G. Daniells.

World War II. Replanting. Reorganizing.

James Lamar McElhany, Senior was a self-taught preacher for the Christian Church. He migrated westward from Arkansas in a wagon train and settled on a 160-acre piece of fertile farmland in the Santa Clara Valley. He married Mary Ford and on January 3, 1880, James Lamar McElhany, Junior was born. After becoming an Adventist Father McElhany took his family of seven northward to Healdsburg, California and in 1887 enrolled in Healdsburg College at the same time that he supported his family as a realtor. Later on several of his children attended the elementary school there.

James Lamar McElhany, Jr. was baptized into the Adventist Church at the age of fifteen by Pastor S. Thurston and in 1900 he enrolled at Healdsburg College for special study. While there he decided to become a minister. He entered denominational employment in 1901 as a colporteur after his year at Healdsburg College, the beginning of fifty-eight years of service for the Seventh-day Adventist Church. On August 3, 1902, he married Cora Belle Ackerman, a nurse from Santa Barbara, California. He worked in the old California Conference and later in the newly organized Southern California Conference.

At the time of the General Conference session held in Oakland in 1903 he was asked to serve in Australia where he was involved in a vigorous program of evangelism. While in Australia he was ordained to the gospel ministry at the New South Wales Camp Meeting of April, 1904. His wife Cora was a soloist and sang while he preached. In 1906 the Philippine Islands needed an ordained minister and James Lamar McElhany, Jr. volunteered to go..

Life was very difficult in the Philippines. When they received a box of fruits and nuts from their family they used the old copies of the *Signs of the Times* that were packed around the fruit to earn extra money.

Cora sold all the copies even though they were outdated and used the cash to purchase food. After two years in the Philippines they went to New Zealand.

When they returned to the States in 1910 Elder McElhany served as a chaplain for a short while at Boulder Sanitarium and pastor of the Boulder church. Then he connected with the Washington Sanitarium and served as chaplain there until June 19, 1913. Then in rapid succession, beginning in 1913, he served as president of the Greater New York Conference, the California Conference, the Southeastern California Conference, the Southern Union Conference, and the Pacific Union Conference.

McElhany was known for his patience, kindness, sympathy, understanding and tact. He was conservative, well-balanced, sincere and had an analytical mind. At the time of the Autumn Council of 1926 he was asked to become the vice president of the General Conference for the North American Division. In 1932 he returned to the Pacific Union Conference for a second brief tenure as president, after which he returned to the world headquarters as a general vice president.

At the General Conference session in 1936, the mantle of chief leader was placed upon his shoulders. He served in this capacity for fourteen years with diligent devotion and strong, efficient leadership. During part of his administration the clouds of World War II hung heavily over the horizon.

During another part of his administration the church was faced with the problems thrust on it by the Great Depression. On August 12, 1939, Elder McElhany lost the companion of his early years and on July 22, 1942, was united in marriage to Matilda Krieger, of Glendale, California.

In 1950 he requested easier responsibilities and he was elected General Conference field secretary and moved his home to California. In his later years cataracts formed over his eyes and he sat in darkness. He was unable to read his Bible but he recalled the precious promises that he had learned while he could see. Surgery corrected the problem and he was happy that he could once again read his Bible. On June 25, 1959, McElhany suffered a stroke and passed away. His body lies in Forest Lawn Cemetery in Glendale, California, not far from the grave site of Arthur G. Daniells.

McElhany was not an impetuous man and gave himself freely to those in distressing situations. One night, in Washington, after he had come from his office, weary with endless committees, and facing more the next day, a young ministerial student knocked at his front door. The student was in deep trouble. Personal problems combined with spiritual doubts plunged him into great mental distress. Elder McElhaney did not send him to his local pastor. He became a pastor of souls himself-ever the minister's highest function-and spent the evening talking with the young man.

More Interesting Facts

*The year 1944 marked the centennial of the 1844 Millerite movement. The Northern New England Conference held a centennial service at the old Washington, New Hampshire church. McElhany was guest speaker for the service on Sabbath and the attendees toured prominent historical places connected with early Seventh-day Adventist pioneers. It was amazing to see how the church had grown in 100 years and how God was leading His people.

*McElhany led the church during the last years of the Great Depression and the even more bitter years of the war that followed. His term of service was during one of the most difficult and bewildering periods in the history of the Adventist Church. One hasty, ill-advised move during any of that time might easily have had repercussions for the Adventist work.

J. L. McElhany

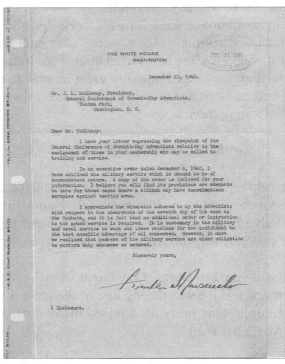

Letter from President Franklin D. Roosevelt responding to McElhany's request for consideration to Adventist noncombatants, dated December 23, 1940.

Left to right: Leslie Ackerman, Belle Ackerman, Luther Ackerman, Cora McElhany, and J. L. McElhany, Etta Ackerman Ross, and David Ross.

J. L. McElhany and wife, Cora with her sister and husband

(Left) Portrait (unlabeled) – believed to be Cora McElhany.
(Right) J. L. McElhany and daughter Esther when she was around two to three years old.

J. L. Mc ELHANY
President of Southern Union Conference

(Left) J. L. McElhany and daughter Esther when she was a young woman of eighteen to twenty years of age.
(Right) J. L. McElhany at the 1922 General Conference Session.

At the end of his term of service, J. L. McElhany welcomes the new president, W. Branson.

McElhany and secretary Meyers in Germany.

McElhany in a meeting in the Inter-American Division.

J. L. McElhany first to sign the temperance pledge after the reorganization of the American Temperance Society. W. A. Sharffenberg, director, looks on.

McElhany grave marker.

Black conferences were formed under McElhany's administration. George E. Peters was the director of the Negro Department and was instrumental in the development of these conferences.

Black delegates and attendees at the 1946 General Conference Session in Takoma Park, Maryland

14. WILLIAM HENRY BRANSON
July 10, 1950-May 24, 1954
(4 years)

Age When Elected President: 62 years old
Church Membership When Elected: 756,712
Secretary: E. D. Dick, D. E. Rebok
Treasurer: C. L. Torrey

Born: August 16, 1887, near Fairfield, Illinois
Died: January 21, 1961, at Glendale, California. He was 73 years old.
Mother: Mary Anne Dicky Branson, store owner
Father: Franklin Parker Branson, carpenter, store owner
Siblings: Jimmie, Martha, Minnie, Joe, William H.
Wife: Married at age 17, Minnie Gertrude Shreve in 1904 (1883-1935)
        In 1936 married Elizabeth Lenora Hinton Robbins, Norfolk, Virginia (1899-1986)
Children: First child died in infancy; Ernest Lloyd, Rachel, Lois Esther Numbers
        Two other children who died early
Ordained: By A. G. Daniells in 1910 at age 23
Church Affiliation of parents: Primitive Baptist
Buried: Montecito Cemetery, Colton, California

South African Division. China. Bible Conference.

On August 16, 1887, Franklin Parker Branson and Mary Anne Dicky Branson became the proud parents of their fifth child, William Henry. Nine years before William's birth some evangelists had come to southern Illinois and held tent meetings. Then when William was six years old some more evangelists conducted meetings in a nearby Adventist Church and the family, except for one son named Joe and Mr. Branson, became Adventists. Mr. Branson remained a Primitive Baptist.

Because Mr. Branson had asthma the family moved near Orlando, Florida, so he could raise cattle and open a store. Young William tried to convince his father of Adventist's truths and developed quite a skill in defending the Bible doctrines as he argued many hours with his father. Early in 1901, at the age of thirteen, William left Florida for school in Battle Creek, Michigan. He was a good cook and earned his expenses by cooking in the Sanitarium kitchen.

Two years later, at age 15, he helped Luther Warren as a tent master in Omaha, Nebraska, and then enrolled in Emmanuel Missionary College at Berrien Springs, Michigan, for one year of schooling. His formal education then stopped except for some correspondence work. He returned to Florida, went to camp meeting and fell in love with a young lady named Minnie Shreve. At age 17, Branson married Minnie and the two began working in a health food restaurant in Salt Lake City, Utah. In 1906 they returned to Florida and he began selling Adventist books door-to-door.

Two years later the Florida Conference asked him to work for them. Will Branson was a good cook and was able to help his wife prepare the meals as their children were added to their household. In later years he often prepared an entire meal for guests. He baked berry cobblers to go along with his baked beans and roasts. Grandson Roy Branson says he still remembers his grandfather's delicious apple pies with a little slice of cheddar cheese on top.

In 1910, A.G. Daniells ordained William H. Branson at the age of twenty-three to the gospel ministry. The next year he became president of the South Carolina Conference. Two years later he transferred to the

Cumberland Conference and became its president. He believed in evangelism and often held evangelistic series while continuing his administrative duties. In 1915, Branson became president of the Southern Union and five years later, the first president of the African Division.

A heavy burden rested on his heart as he contemplated how to reach the millions of unsaved people in the beautiful countries of Africa. He traveled all over into the remotest areas by train, boat, bicycle and foot making plans to establish mission schools and churches. He kept accurate notes on the needs and progress of mission development and his conversations with village chiefs. Everywhere he went he preached and encouraged the nationals to accept Jesus. On May 29, 1923, Branson and a few others left South Africa, headed north, determined to enter the Belgian Congo and open a mission station. Many of the streams had no bridges and Branson had to be carried over piggyback by some of the native porters. Branson weighed well over 200 pounds and several times he was dropped into the muddy streams.

Branson chronicled his many travels and experiences in Africa in several books: *Missionary Adventures in Africa,* (1925); and *Pioneering in the Lion Country*, (1938). His books stirred many young people to respond to the call of taking the gospel light to Africa. In 1930 he was called to the General Conference as a vice-president with special emphasis on the African Division where he had worked so long.

Branson had strong personal convictions on many issues, and when he thought he was right he had the courage to battle for his position. When Faith for Today, the television broadcast, almost stopped because the General Conference budget committee did not vote funds for its continuance, Branson loyally championed it. He knew it would advance the work of the church.

Branson was a tireless worker but he enjoyed life. He found pleasure in boating and fishing and owned a cabin by the beach where he kept his boat and outboard motor. Gardening and doing small chores about the house brought him great joy. He loved camping in the open air, cooking all of his food on a campfire and sleeping under the stars.

After thirty-one years of marriage, his wife Minnie Shreve Branson died. He later married Elizabeth Hinton Robbins in 1936. Elizabeth traveled with him in 1938 when he assumed direction of the China Division. China was going through a period of great perplexity and increasing communism and it needed very wise leadership. China was closing its doors to foreigners and missionaries had to live under difficult conditions. The Church needed Branson's wise leadership in this area at that time. In 1950 at the General Conference session in San Francisco he was elected president of the world church. Branson was an able chairman, full of ideas and always attentive to the details and organization.

In September, 1952, Elder Branson was responsible for a special Bible conference that convened in Takoma Park, Maryland. It had been thirty-three years since a similar conference on the Bible had been convened. There were eighty-two presentations with a devotional lecture each day at noon. Sabbath services were open to the public. The meeting commenced with a communion service on Friday afternoon and a revival church service on Sabbath. The leaders set a goal to double church membership from 1950 to 1953. This could only be done if there was revival among church leaders. They also felt that a whole new generation of leaders had come into the church that could benefit by a series of revival messages centered on Bible study.

Furthermore, a re-examination of doctrinal positions would help make sure that they were setting forth the truth in a way that most fully explained the meaning of the times. In addition, the events surrounding World War II caused Adventist prophetic expositors to re-examine some points of prophetic exposition. The 1952 Bible Conference paved the way for new scholarly projects like the *Seventh-day Adventist Bible Commentary* (published 1953-1957) and *Problems in Bible Translation* (1954).

The edited transcripts of the 1952 conference were published as *Our Firm Foundation* in 1953. The conference helped unite the Seventh-day Adventist Churches throughout the world. By the close of

Branson's four-year term as president, Parkinson's disease had begun to affect his health and he resigned from his post at the 1954 General Conference session.

In his last sermon to the delegates Elder Branson urged them to move forward in the activity he loved most–evangelism. "The whole business of the church is to save souls. No sermon speaks as it should unless it is evangelistic. Jesus is coming again. We must sing it; we must preach it; we must believe it; and we must constantly be ready for it." William H. Branson died January 21, 1961, just about a month after his son, Elder Ernest L. Branson, passed away.

More Interesting Facts

*Branson's red hair intrigued the people of Africa. They had seen many white men with black hair, white hair, blonde hair and other colors, but they had never seen anybody with hair as red as his. They thought his hair indicated that he was a big chief.

*While looking for places to establish mission stations in Africa he traveled by foot, bicycle, boat and rail, most of the time sleeping and eating out in the open air by a campfire.

*His son, Ernest Lloyd Branson, was an outstanding missionary and leader in the Middle East, and president of the Greater New York Conference.

*Roy Branson, his grandson, has been an active educator, mentor, ethicist, and advocate for social justice for many decades and has been on the faculty of Washington Adventist University and Loma Linda University. He received his PhD in Religious Ethics from Harvard University in 1968 and co-founded *Spectrum* magazine.

*Bruce Branson, M.D., another grandson, was Chair of the Loma Linda University School of Medicine surgery department that supervised the training of all the surgery residents and simultaneously served as Chief of Surgery at the LLU Medical Center. He was sent by Dr. Hinshaw to be the first faculty physician from White Memorial Hospital to go to Loma Linda when the clinical teaching was transferred from White Memorial to Loma Linda. Bruce was also chair of the committee that visited medical schools/centers around the country that recommended the clover-leaf configuration of circular towers that is LLU's distinctive architectural design.

Ronald L. Numbers, another of W. H. Branson's grandsons, in 1976 wrote *Prophetess of Health* which rejected Ellen White's special revelation and inspiration and tried to show that Mrs. White depended on other contemporary sources for information and had covered up this borrowing. Numbers taught at Andrews and Loma Linda Universities, but at the time he published his book he was employed at the University of Wisconsin.

*W. H. Branson also wrote *The Way to Christ, The Holy Spirit, In Defense of the Faith, How Men are Saved* and *Drama of the Ages*.

Helderberg College (1893), the first College of the Seventh-day Adventist Church established outside the United States, named the administration building "Branson Hall" in honor of Branson who was president of the South African Division at the time when the college moved to its present site in 1928. The Branson Site of North York General Hospital in Toronto, Ontario, Canada, is named for Branson. Originally the Seventh-day Adventist Hospital and then North York Branson Hospital, it was amalgamated with the public North York General Hospital during a period of hospital consolidations in Ontario in 1997.

(Left) Branson about 1945
(Right) William H. Branson

"Ever since Elders C. L. Bauer and M. V. Campbell came to our room in our hotel about 6 P.M. today and told Mrs. Branson and me of the action of the nominating committee, we have been overwhelmed. I have always had very high ideals regarding the type of man who should stand as the leader of God's people, and especially in these last days of peril and of final preparation for our Lord's return. But I have never felt that I could personally measure up to that standard. I feel that I am the least of the apostles. I have no natural abilities to carry such a task as you have asked me to carry. I see so much of weakness and faultiness in my life that I shrink from undertaking this holy task. One thing is sure, I have no confidence in the flesh. Of mine own self I can do nothing. I have, however, always believed in our constituted committees and have felt that their calls should be heeded…When the brethren left our hotel room, Mrs. Branson and I fell upon our knees and pleaded with God to forgive us our sins and make us what we ought to be and the kind of people God's church expects its leaders to be. Only God can be my sufficiency. My trust shall be in Him. I am fully persuaded that this is His people and that we have His truth and that He will lead us. It is because of my absolute confidence in His leadership of His church upon the earth that I find courage to undertake this great task. I plead for all of you to pray for me, for I shall always need your earnest prayers. I know that I shall have your cooperation, and this too gives me courage. My chief burden shall be the winning of souls. This, I believe, should be our greatest of all goals. Our chief business as a church is to make ready a people prepared for the Lord."

W. H Branson, *Review and Herald*, July 13, 1950, p. 48

Branson at the Landow church in 1947

Roy Branson, grandson

Roy Branson in front of *Spectrum* logo, the magazine he helped found.

Grave marker of wife, Elizabeth Robbins Branson

Branson and W. R. Beach at Walla Walla College.

Branson at a meeting in Switzerland. He is second from right.

Bible and History Teacher's Council, 1919, Takoma Park, MD. Daniells in center and Branson third from right.

(Left) Ernest L. Branson, the son, and leader in the Middle East and New York.
(Right) During the China Division program at the General Conference session, Mrs. Branson poses with some children dressed in Chinese costumes: From left: Carol Anne Miller, Robin Winter, Tommie Miller.

Branson missionary family. Left: Ernest L. Branson (President of Middle East Union), his wife and son;
Right: Raymond W. Numbers (President of British West Indies Union), his wife (Lois Branson) Numbers and two children;
Center: Elder and Mrs. W. H. Branson. Picture from *Review and Herald*, 7/16/50, p. 93

After the death of his first wife, Minnie Shreve Branson, Elder Branson married
Elizabeth Robbins pictured here with her son, Jack.

Branson funeral at the Loma Linda Church.

Elder B. W. Abney in 1931 as a missionary to South Africa with his family: Mrs. Celia M. Abney, son Benjamin, and daughter Celia (Cleveland). Elder Branson was present at Oakwood College when the student body and faculty gave this family a touching farewell. Branson remarked "the going out of Elder Abney and his family to the great African field as missionaries to that land, really marks a new era in the history of this school."

15. REUBEN RICHARD FIGUHR
May 24, 1954-June 16, 1966
(12 years)

Age when elected president: 57 years old
Church Membership When Elected: 972,071
Secretary: W. R. Beach
Treasurer: C. L. Torrey

Born: October 20, 1896, in West Superior, Wisconsin
Died: October 28, 1983, at Napa, California. He was 87 years old.
Mother: Julia Remiche. Their ancestors were from the German immigrants who migrated to Russia during the 1700's, settling in the Province of Volynia, near Kiev.
Father: Jacob E. Figuhr
Siblings: Lizzie, Rupert, Harry, Lydia, Rueben, Hattie, Lillian Wright
Wife: July 4, 1918, married May Belle Holt, a school teacher, four days before he was inducted into the US Army at age 21.
Ordained: June 18, 1918 by H. W. Cottrell
Education: Thatuma Junior Academy; Laurelwood Academy, 1916; Pacific Union College; Walla Walla College, B. A. 1922
Church Affiliation of parents: Moravian Brethren Church. Mrs. Figuhr and her sister were baptized secretly at night by Pastor Hermann because their husbands opposed their joining the church
Buried: Saint Helena Public Cemetery, Saint Helena, California

Philippines. Cautious and deliberate. Walter Martin.

Reuben Richard Figuhr was born October 20, 1896, in West Superior, Wisconsin. His German ancestors had migrated to Russia during the 1700s and settled near Kiev. They heard about the economic opportunities in America and they left Russia while hidden under hay in a produce wagon and crossed the Atlantic Ocean in steerage class, the very cheapest form of ocean travel. When they arrived in America they settled in Wisconsin close to relatives who had left the year before.

Shortly thereafter the teachings of the Seventh-day Adventist Church came to the family through brochures printed in German. They were members of the Moravian Brethren Church and it was very difficult to leave their fellowship. Reuben Figuhr's mother and her sister had to be baptized secretly by Pastor Hermann.

Mrs. Figuhr wanted her four children to attend Adventist schools so she moved to Idaho, then to Oregon. Reuben arrived unannounced at the nearest town, left his suitcase at the small railroad station, and started out on foot in search of Laurelwood Academy. After walking for a long time and being on the verge of despair he was about to turn around when he saw a pretty young lady about his own age coming down the road. He inquired about the Academy and she told him that it was just a short distance away and she added that her name was May Holt.

Reuben found Laurelwood Academy and graduated in 1916. May Holt, the pretty young lady who had given him directions had become a schoolteacher. Reuben helped in various tent efforts and taught elementary school before the United States Army called him. Four days before his induction into the United States Army, he married May Belle Holt in a home wedding in Portland, Oregon, on July 4, 1918.

On June 19, 1918, he was ordained by H.W. Cottrell, the same minister who would marry him. After just four months in the Army the war ended and Ruben returned to civilian life. He did a year of study at

Pacific Union College and then transferred to Walla Walla College where he received his B.A. degree in 1922 with a major in history. Reuben Figuhr was asked to go to the Philippines and he and his wife May arrived there in May, 1923. He taught school and was the acting dean of boys and in the meantime had to learn the local language, Tagalog.

Figuhr prepared three sermons with his limited knowledge of Tagalog and without an interpreter made a trip to a number of the rural churches. When he had preached three sermons in one place he went to the next church and repeated them. Eventually he became superintendent of the Philippine Union Conference. He and his wife made many sacrifices so that the message would go forward. When he had to travel by bus or train he always went by third class.

Pastor Figuhr lived with the local people and ate their food. When he traveled he carried a mat, a mosquito net and a double sheet with him. At bedtime he put the mat on the floor, spread the sheets so that he could use half as the cover, and slept soundly under the mosquito net. He oversaw the building of the Manila Sanitarium and Hospital, the development of the Philippine Union College and many church schools and academies.

Mrs. Figuhr served as the Union Sabbath School Secretary, taught music, conducted choirs and held cooking schools. In 1941 Reuben became the president of the South American Division and their two children (Richard Allen, born in Washington State, and Wilma Jean, born in the Philippines) entered school at Pacific Union College while their parents lived at division headquarters in Buenos Aires, Argentina.

Reuben Figuhr emphasized health instruction, strengthened literature evangelism, and pushed the educational program. He also studied a new language- Spanish. He now had a working knowledge of four languages-English, German, Tagalog, and Spanish. His philosophy of frugality permeated the entire headquarters and division. His emphasis on the economy allowed the mission fields to develop and expand under his guidance.

In 1950 Reuben Figuhr was selected general vice president of the General Conference and in 1954 at the General Conference session in San Francisco, he was elected world leader of the Seventh-day Adventist Church. As president, he announced the policy that would mark his administration: "I just want to say that I wish to be found in the middle of the road, walking toward the kingdom of God." It is said that his little granddaughter promptly pronounced with genuine concern, "But he'll get run over if he does that, won't he?"

Over the years the divided campus of the denomination's medical school with one part in Los Angeles and the other at Loma Linda 60 miles away had created increasing problems. He supported the recommendation that the medical school be located on the Loma Linda campus and laid plans for a school of dentistry to be a part of the medical school.

When Walter Martin, a specialist in cults, planned a book about Adventists, Figuhr was instrumental in setting up a committee with scholars and authors to produce the 700-page book *Questions on Doctrine* which answered the demand for the history and beliefs of the Seventh-day Adventist Church. The discussions lasted for eighteen months and clarified both for the Adventists and non-Adventists the beliefs of the Adventist Church and established the fact that Adventism was not a cult.

Walter Martin wrote that Adventists were "born-again Christians and truly brethren in Christ." Then Walter Martin and Dr. Barnhouse, the editor of *Eternity* magazine published a series of articles on Adventism. They argued that Adventists "held many strange views at odds with orthodox Christianity, yet on the essentials of the deity of Christ, the sinfulness of man and the efficacy of the atonement, the basic SDA teaching was within the bounds of Biblical orthodoxy." More than one sixth of the approximately 35,000 *Eternity* subscribers cancelled their subscriptions in protest.

Elder Figuhr was cautious, guarded, deliberate, devoted, focused. He served the church faithfully guided by the Bible and the Spirit of Prophecy for forty-seven years and retired in 1966.

More Interesting Facts

*Their son, Dr. Richard Figuhr, served as president of Canadian Union College and his wife, Ann Stump Figuhr, was a concert pianist.

*Granddaughter, Rae Lee Cooper, a nurse and musician, is married to Lowell Cooper, a General Conference Vice President.

*Daughter Wilma Jean married a preacher, Alva R. Appel (1922-2006), who was Chief of Chaplains for the United States Air Force Auxiliary Civil Air Patrol (CAP), Chaplain Colonel of the United States Congressional Squadron, and a strong climber who looked for Noah's ark.

*The Seventh-day Adventist Church reached its first million members in 1955. It took 92 years. Today, it adds a million new members every year.

(Left) Reuben R. Figuhr, fifteenth president of the Seventh-day Adventist Church
(Right) May Belle Holt Figuhr, wife of Elder R.R. Figuhr

Dr. Richard A. Figuhr, son of the Figuhrs

Grandson, Richard Allen Figuhr, Jr., was killed in an army ambulance helicopter accident in England at age 21.

Granddaughter Rae Lee Figuhr Cooper and Lowell Cooper

R. R. Figuhr and his Thatuna Academy 12th grade graduating class. Figuhr is rear, far left.
Thatuna Academy, in Viola, Idaho, had closed by 1915.

Wedding of Rae Lee Figuhr and Lowell Cooper June 11, 1967, at the College Church at Lacombe, Alberta, Canada. Rae Lee's father and mother, Dr. and Mrs. R.A. Figuhr, are standing at the top and her grandparents, Elder and Mrs. R. R. Figuhr are standing at the bottom.

Grave marker of the Figuhrs

Reuben R. Figuhr, Percy W. Christian, and Bob F. Correis examine some treasures from the mission field.

Elder Figuhr giving a lecture.

(Left) Figuhr welcomes Frank L. Peterson, first black vice president of the General Conference.
(Right) Retiring president R. R. Figuhr greets Anna Knight first black missionary to India now 95 years old.

San Francisco Mayor, George Christopher, declares July 27, 1962, as Seventh–day Adventist Day in San Francisco.
Here Mayor Christopher, at his desk in city hall, signs the official proclamation. President R. R. Figuhr looks on, holding the
key to the city which the mayor had presented a few moments earlier as a symbol of San Francisco's
good will toward the Adventists.

Dollis Pierson, wife of incoming president pins a farewell rose on Mrs. Figuhr, retiring first lady.

Outgoing president Figuhr and incoming president Pierson face the future together.

16. ROBERT HOWARD PIERSON
June 16, 1966-January 3, 1979

(12 years)

Age When Elected President: 55 years old
Church Membership When Elected: 1,661,657
Secretary: W. R. Beach, Clyde O. Franz
Treasurer: K. H. Emmerson

Born: January 3, 1911, in Brooklyn, Iowa
Died: January 21, 1989, in Kailua, Hawaii. He was 78 years old.
Baptized: Baptized at the age of 13 in Ocala, Florida
Mother: Mable Johnson Pierson
Father: Will G. Pierson, president of the Poweshiek County Bank, businessman and realtor
Siblings: Fifth and youngest child of the family; Robin, Ruth, John, Genevieve, Robert.
Wife: Married Dollis Mae Smith, September 2, 1931, a schoolteacher.
Children: Dr. John Duane Pierson, Collegedale, Tennessee (physician)
　　　　　Dr. Robert George Pierson, Surat, India (has his degree in geography)
Ordained: Poona, India, 1936
Education: Southern Missionary College; May 29, 1966, Honorary D.D. from Andrews University
Church Affiliation of parents: Mother a third generation Adventist, father a Methodist
Retirement: January 3, 1979
Buried: Shepherd Memorial Park, Henderson, North Carolina

Athlete. Poet. Evangelist.

Robert Pierson was not a "bad boy" growing up but he had not fully committed himself to Christ. His main focus was sports. He didn't have time in his heart for Christ or the church. At Summerfield High he was captain of the football team and captain of the track team. He played basketball in the winter, baseball in the spring, football in the fall, and swam in the summer. He had to walk five miles to school and five miles back to his house so he was always in good shape. When he could he would do a little boxing on the side.

Born on January 3, 1911, in the small town of Brooklyn, Iowa, he was surrounded with the love of a Christian family. His mother was a third-generation Seventh-day Adventist (her grandmother had been baptized by Elder A. G. Daniells) and she led out in daily family worship. She called all five of her children by name and prayed, "Dear Lord, save all of us as an *unbroken family* in Thy kingdom."

Mrs. Pierson had a disfigured left arm and hand that would not open fully. Before Robert's birth, a kerosene stove had exploded in the kitchen, setting the frame house on fire. His mother got burned as she ran from the kitchen, yet she ran back into the flames to rescue her firstborn child. Covering the child with her own body, she had stumbled back out of the fire so badly injured that she was in and out of the hospital for a year. Every one of her children knew that she would sacrifice her life for them and they loved and respected their religious mother.

Robert's father was a member of the Methodist Church but he didn't interfere with the way Mrs. Pierson raised her children. He was president of the Poweshiek County Bank until the Depression came in the 1930s and closed down the smaller banks. At that time he moved his family from Iowa to Florida where he entered real estate. Mr. Pierson was a good businessman and insisted that his children have savings accounts and that each one earn money by mowing lawns and selling milk or cottage cheese.

Already Robert was being recognized for his writing abilities and he was selected to be the editor of the high school paper and at the age of twelve had one of his poems published in the *Brooklyn (Iowa) Chronicle*. He became a prolific writer, both of prose and poetry.

It was when he turned twenty that he committed himself to his mother's church and her faith. He received a telegram from Florida where his parents were living requesting him to come quickly because his mother was critically ill. He had plenty of time to reflect on the influence his mother had had on him as he drove from Iowa to Florida. He remembered how happy she had been at his baptism at the age of thirteen into the Ocala, Florida, Seventh-day Adventist Church.

He needed to tell his mother how much he loved her and appreciated her Christian love. He wanted to tell her how much he had appreciated her prayers and that they were not in vain for him. When he arrived at her home in Bellevue, Florida, his mother was in a coma and he was unable to tell her how much her daily prayers had meant to him. He went into the next room and wept with an open Bible before him. He pledged himself to follow his mother's faith and go wherever Christ would have him go.

The Holy Spirit urged him into the ministry. He married his high school sweetheart, Dollis Mae Smith, a young schoolteacher, in Ocala, Florida, on September 2, 1931, and immediately following the wedding they left by car and matriculated at Southern Missionary College (Southern Adventist University) at Collegedale, Tennessee. Robert got a job milking cows at the college dairy which forced him to get up at three o'clock in the morning to hand-milk his twelve cows. He would then rush home and change clothes for his classes and then rush back to the barn to milk his twelve cows again. In between the studies and the work to pay for their schooling Robert was able to conduct an evangelistic effort in a nearby town. Fifteen people accepted the Bible truths he taught and soon a church of twenty-five members was organized.

When he graduated in 1933 he was asked to become a pastor-teacher in Columbus, Georgia. Pastor Pierson learned here how to activate church members to work together and plan together and accomplish great things for the Lord together. Pastor Pierson and Dollis learned to work together and help each other. He shared the teaching duties and Dollis helped with Bible studies and evangelistic meetings. In those depression days they had a combined salary of $65 per month but they managed. Each weekday morning Dollis taught the thirteen church school pupils while Robert prepared sermons and radio programs. He supervised their son John's care in the morning. Dollis came home at noon, and Robert went to teach the afternoon classes at the church school. They had Bible studies and evangelistic meetings in the evenings.

In just a year he was made Home Missionary Secretary of the Georgia-Cumberland Conference. After one year at this post they left for India. Two and one half years after entering denominational employment Robert Pierson was ordained to the gospel ministry in Poona, India, in 1936. He was constantly asked for materials from preachers on building sermons. He developed a file system with some 700 subjects by using an envelope-and-card filing system with cross references. The system enabled him to prepare a 2500 word sermon every day when he would have a radio program in New York City and still have time to care for the large amount of correspondence that he had to answer. He had a great ability to lead, to select, to train, and to inspire men to achieve new goals.

"Thousands may not hear my preaching,
Masses may my witness shun,
Give me, then, the single sinner-
Help me, Lord, to win just one!"

This was the poem that he wrote after arriving in India in 1935 and seeing the great multitudes of people.

Elder Pierson would frequently begin writing before 5 o'clock in the morning. Once his busy day began it was impossible to write. People were constantly coming to his office asking for help. He learned to use every spare minute, Sundays, while waiting in hotel rooms and in airports and on airplanes. His biography *Radiant with Hope* shows him to be the author of twenty-eight books. Many of his articles appeared in denominational papers like the *Review and Herald*, the *Youth's Instructor* and *Ministry* magazine.

Pierson was recognized as an outstanding administrator. In 1939 he became president of the South India Conference and later the South India Union. Then he served as president of the British West Indies Union, president of the Caribbean Union, president of the Southern Asia Division, president of the Kentucky-Tennessee Conference, president of the Texas Conference, president of the Trans-Africa Division and finally president of the General Conference.

As General Conference president, Pierson appealed to the laity and leadership of the denomination to hold fast to the church's fundamental beliefs, including the doctrine of the work of Jesus Christ as High Priest in the heavenly sanctuary, and the concept of the true believers overcoming all their sins with the aid of God. In October, 1978, he shocked the Annual Council by announcing that he would resign (or retire) from the presidency effective on his birthday (January 3, 1979). His doctors had told him that his health was not good and that he was facing the risk of a stroke due to the relentless pressures of his presidency.

Once he was released from the pressure of the presidency his health began to improve and he began to accept appointments in different places. Although he turned seventy-eight on January 3, 1989, he and his wife Dollis accepted an invitation to serve as interim pastor of the Kailua church on the island of Oahu. Just a few weeks into their two month assignment Elder Pierson suffered a massive heart attack. He awoke early in the morning with discomfort in his chest and left arm.

The physician friend and houseguest was summoned and insisted that he go to the emergency room of the nearby Castle Medical Center. Moments later Elder Pierson was observed kneeling in prayer. Shortly he collapsed, and all resuscitative efforts failed. He died on his knees on Sabbath morning (January 21) in Hawaii. Elder Pierson spent forty-six years in ministry, with another ten in service after retirement. Of the forty-six years of service, twenty-five were spent in overseas posts.

About 1000 people came to pay tribute to the former General Conference president who called the church to revival and reformation. The funeral was held in Henderson, North Carolina, on January 26 and he was laid to rest in the Shepherd Memorial Park. The Pierson's had two sons; Dr. John Duane, a physician and Dr. Robert George, an educational administrator. Dollis Pierson, who married her high school sweetheart on September 2, 1931, and accompanied him for forty-six years, passed away in Fletcher Park, North Carolina, on November 8, 2005, at age 94.

More Interesting Facts

*Elder Pierson had several brushes with death in his work. Once he found himself over the Caribbean in an aged PBX seaplane that was held together by "bailing wire and the eleventh chapter of Hebrews," its radio dead and its compass gone. Another time he was adrift with the sharks off Devil's Island. On a return trip from the first camp meeting ever held for the Davis Indians, he was washed over the Ituwubai Falls in British Guyana.

Once while he was in the Congo he was caught between enemy fire on the mission compound in Elizabethville (now Lubumbashi). Twenty-nine missionaries found shelter under tables and beds as heavy machine gun fire smashed windows and shattered doors. When the gunfire slowed down Pierson rushed to his guest room to get some of his personal items. As he reached to open the closet, a terrific explosion shook the room. Debris tumbled around him, filling the air with dust, smoke, and plaster. Water gushed from a burst pipe as a bazooka shell scored a direct hit on the bathroom. A piece of shrapnel passed a foot from his head.

After being under heavy fire for fifty-two hours, the missionaries decided that it was time to escape. They had special prayer and while they were praying a knock came on the door. The president of the mission announced that a plane was ready to take the visitors out. God protected them as they drove to the airport between enemy fire and heavily-armed soldiers.

Robert and Dollis Pierson in 1974

Robert Pierson

(Left) Elder and Mrs. Pierson chat with a church member
(Right) Elder Pierson congratulates Elinor Wilson

Pierson, Emmerson and Franz, president, treasurer and secretary

Pierson baptizes his grandson

Dr. Robert G. Pierson, son.

The Wilsons are welcomed by Elder R. H. Pierson.

While visiting the Congo, the Union office where Elder Pierson was staying was attacked and damaged.

The Congo missionaries crossing the border into Zambia.

One of the damaged windows.

Damage done to the Congo mission compound.

A shell left after the attack at the Congo compound.

The Congo mission office.

(Left) Mrs. Dollis Pierson.
(Rightt) Mrs. Pierson doing office work

(Left) Elder and Mrs. Pierson
(Right) Dollis Pierson and Del Delker at the 1980 General Conference session in Dallas, Texas

(Left) Mrs. Pierson doing some missionary work.
(Right) Pierson seeking the Lord in prayer

Robert and Dollis Pierson

17. NEAL CLAYTON WILSON
January 3, 1979-July 5, 1990
(11 years)

Age When Elected President: 58 years old
Church Membership When Elected: 3,300,181
Secretary: Clyde O. Franz, G. Ralph Thompson
Treasurer: K. H. Emmerson, L. L. Butler, Donald F. Gilbert

Born: July 5, 1920; in Lodi, California
Died: December 14, 2010, in Dayton, Maryland. He was 90 years old.
Baptized: 1935
Mother: Hannah Wallin Wilson, teacher, book keeper
Father: Nathaniel Carter Wilson, pastor and administrator
Siblings: Clarice June Wilson Woodward, June 7, 1922, Stockton, California
       Ruth Elvira Wilson Murrill, November 12, 1925, Lusaka, Zambia
       Wilbur Bruce Wilson, March 16, 1934, Bloemfontein, South Africa
       Donald Wallin Wilson, January 9, 1938, Poona, India; died May 16, 2003
Wife: July 19, 1942 married Elinor Neumann from Chicago
Children: Ted N. C. Wilson
       Shirley Wilson
Ordained: February 26, 1944; Elder James McElhany preached ordination sermon
Education: B. A., Pacific Union College; June 5, 1977, D. D. Andrews University
Church Affiliation of parents: Neal's grandfather, William Henry Wilson, joined the Adventist Church at a California camp meeting in 1904 when Ellen G. White made an appeal. He had not been interested in religion before that.
Buried: Ft. Lincoln Cemetery in Brentwood, Maryland

Superb chairman. Statesman. Climbed Mt. Kilimanjaro.

Nathaniel Carter Wilson married Hannah Wallin on October 1, 1919, and to this union five children were born. The oldest, Neal Clayton Wilson, was born on July 5, 1920, in Lodi, California. Elder Nathaniel Wilson, a church administrator and missionary, began his work as the Bible teacher at Madison College. Neal and his sister Clarice had a normal family life on the farm at Madison, Tennessee.

In 1925 the family left for Africa. Neal was nearly five, Clarice two and Ruth was born shortly after they arrived in Africa. Their mother, Hannah, was their first and only teacher for their early years. She homeschooled them in Lusaka and Blantyre. Hannah was a strict disciplinarian and saw to it that the children kept their heads in the books yet allowed them enough time to play outdoors and experiment with nature.

Elder Wilson moved to Cape Town in 1929 where for a short time Neal and Clarice attended their first formal school at Claremont Union College which would later become Helderberg College. Later when they moved to Bloemfontein, Neal attended an all boy's school, Grey College. Neal probably developed an interest in sports while at Grey College from 1930-1934. Grey College was known for its sporting excellence.

While on furlough Neal and Clarice attended Lodi Academy for the 1934-35 school year. Neal would follow in the footsteps of his father and uncles by attending their Alma Mater, Lodi Academy.

Neal was coming into full manhood and found sports to be his new interest. He devoted every spare moment to this challenging activity. He became involved in track and field, polo, soccer, mountaineering, swimming and other sports. The next year when the Wilsons went to India, his shelves and walls were decorated with medals, ribbons, trophies, cups and pictures reminding him of his athletic ability.

The 15-year-old lanky youth really felt proud when he won a national title in the regional sport of badminton in the Western Indian Championship. And then something happened that made him really think about his future; he was struck with infantile paralysis (polio). For weeks he drifted in and out of high fever and delirium. The doctors gave him up for dead.

He made a covenant with the Lord in the dark of that sickroom. He would do something other than wait for the sound of those applauding his sport's achievements. He would learn to do something for human beings that had a more enduring, lasting nature.

His mother applied hot and cold packs to his legs for several weeks until his full strength returned. Even in later life, his family says one of his legs was weaker than the other. But he still had tremendous strength even in the weaker leg. Sports were no longer the consuming passion of his life. He got out of bed in India and knew he had a new direction for his life. He wanted to do things that would help prepare him for serving others. At his baptism in 1935 he gave his heart fully to Christ and the Church.

Neal and Clarice attended Vincent Hill School and College from March, 1936, until the end of the school year in November, 1939. Vincent Hill School and College agreed with Neal. He was chosen as president of his junior college senior class, and looked forward to graduation. The class members spent a great deal of time on speeches and plans for graduation which took place Saturday night, November 25 (1939). He had to give the President's address and would sing in a mixed quartet. Clarice would give the farewell address. Neal's grades were excellent. He was among those who averaged above 90% for the fifth period of 1939. He also played the trumpet and trombone in the school orchestra and took a course in the Fundamentals of Hymnology. He indicated that he personally owned his trumpet and trombone.

The Wilson family left India in 1940 and Neal and Clarice enrolled in Pacific Union College (PUC). The two years that Neal spent at PUC finishing his Bachelor's degree were busy ones. In addition to his classes, he was a staff member of the school newspaper and participated in the *Campus Chronicle* subscription campaign.

An attractive young lady by the name of Elinor Neumann from Chicago admired the tall, thin, college boy who served salads in the Sanitarium dining room and was pleased when he started stopping by the San store where she worked. This attractive young lady and her family had a very interesting history. Her mother, Theresa Werderich Neumann, had emigrated to America around 1912 from Austria.

Nineteen forty-two was a big year for Neal. He graduated on May 17, 1942 from Pacific Union College with his Bachelor of Arts Degree in Religion with minors in history and speech, and began his internship in Wyoming on June 1, 1942, at a salary of $18.00 per week.

The biggest event of the year was his marriage to Elinor on July 19, 1942. The marriage started out humbly. Elinor had $300 to her name and paid for the wedding. Neal had $300 and bought a car-and that was enough to begin life together.

The newlywed couple drove to Sheridan, Wyoming, and Neal went right to work in the Wyoming field in a summer evangelistic effort. Four days after their marriage a letter arrived asking them to consider leaving their work in Wyoming to go into mission service. It informed them of the Church's plan for the preparation of ten missionaries for work in Arabic fields and requested they come to Washington for Arabic language study.

On Sabbath afternoon, February 26, 1944, a very unusual service was conducted in Columbia Hall of Washington Missionary College when ten young workers, all trained to work in Arabic fields, were ordained to the gospel ministry. Elder McElhany, the world church president, preached the sermon. Neal and Elinor Wilson boarded a Portuguese steamer in Philadelphia and sailed for Alexandria, Egypt, the next day – Sunday, February 27, 1944.

Although he was called to Egypt to be a pastor and evangelist, when the leaders saw Neal's enthusiasm and zeal for the work he was appointed superintendent of the Egyptian Mission very quickly in addition to those responsibilities. Early in 1945 Neal Wilson had an overwhelming conviction to start a school that would train Egyptian young people. This Egypt Training School (later called the Nile Union Academy and the Adventist Theological Institute of Egypt) was moved in 1954 to Gabal el-Asfar near Heliopolis. When in the mid-1950s government curriculum requirements caused the church to close most of it schools, this school, along with the Heliopolis Adventist School, remained open.

Neal and Elinor had been married for nearly eight years when they discovered that Elinor was expecting their first child. Since Elinor was pregnant they requested their furlough. It was granted beginning April 1, 1950. Neal's sister, Ruth Murrill, was teaching nursing at Washington Sanitarium and Hospital and it was decided that the "San" would be the best place for the delivery. Elinor had the baby, Norman Clair (Ted), almost as soon as they arrived from Egypt on May 10, 1950. Their second child, Shirley Jean, was born in Cairo, on January 24, 1953.

After a few years of experience in Central California, Neal was called to the Columbia Union. Neal Wilson was now 39 years old and took up his new work on February 1, 1960. He would be the new secretary for the Religious Liberty and Medical Departments as well as the Association of Self-Supporting Institutions (ASI) for the Columbia Union. He soon became president of the Columbia Union.

In 1966 Seventh-day Adventists from around the world converged on Detroit, Michigan, for the 50th session of the General Conference. On Friday afternoon the delegates ratified the nomination of Robert H. Pierson and on Monday afternoon, June 20, 1966, the rest of the report of the nominating committee was heard and voted on. Neal C. Wilson had been elected vice president of the General Conference for North America, replacing Theodore Carcich.

Neal Wilson proved to be an indefatigable worker surviving on five hours of sleep on most nights. At the Annual Council of the General Conference Monday morning, October 16, 1978, after the morning devotional, Pastor Pierson announced that he must retire. His doctors warned that unless he was relieved of his heavy responsibilities, the risk of a stroke would be high.

This was the first time that a president had resigned between sessions and leaders were not quite sure what to do. A special nominating committee was set up to study the situation and it recommended Neal Wilson to fill out the term as president of the General Conference effective January 3, 1979, (Pierson's birthday when he would leave).

Neal Wilson was at home in Africa, India, South America, Russia or any other part of the world. Because he had lived so much of his life outside of the United States he felt comfortable wherever he was and with any group of people. He represented the church with dignity and grace as he met heads of state and political leaders. Whether meeting President Ronald Reagan, ambassadors, congressmen, or mayors, he was always a capable statesman. He championed the cause of temperance and on many occasions met leaders who were interested in promoting a better life for their citizens. He had a photographic memory with names and once he had met you, you were his friend forever.

N. C. Wilson made a great committee chairman. He relished committees and mastered the agenda. He studied and prepared for every item, becoming thoroughly versed in the pros and cons, options, nuances, concerns, and anxieties. If a major matter came up for consideration, Wilson always took the chair and when he was in the chair, the committee did not break. You had to make your own arrangements to get a drink or visit the restroom. Wilson wouldn't budge all morning, all afternoon, or through a long night session. Committee members humorously remarked to one another that he was like a camel.

In 1980, at the General Conference session held in Dallas, Texas, Wilson had no trouble at all being reelected to the presidency. The year and a half he had served as president of the world church gave ample evidence of his dedication and skill as the leader of the church. He was reelected in record time. At the 1985 General Conference session in New Orleans, Louisiana, Neal Wilson was again reelected.

Thursday, July 5, 1990, was an important day for Neal Wilson. It was his 70th birthday. It was also important because as president of the world church he had to give the keynote address to the delegates assembled in the Hoosier Dome for the 55th Session of the General Conference. It was also important because as the incumbent president he had to be reelected here to serve for the next five- year term of service. No one foresaw any problems with his reelection. Wilson's health was good. His mind was sharp and his leadership was still dynamic. It was a very good day.

However, the nominating committee considered Wilson's age and the fact he had led the North American Division and the General Conference for a combined total of twenty-four years and concluded that they needed a change in leadership and a younger leader. George Brown was nominated first, but refused to accept the position and then the committee selected Robert Folkenberg.

The sun set for good on the life of Neal Clayton Wilson on December 14, 2010. The memorial service was held a month later in the General Conference auditorium in Silver Spring, Maryland, on January 19, 2011, at 2:00 PM. The beautiful and touching two-and-one-half-hour service was filled with music and laughter, tears and reflections, preaching and speeches. It was a fitting tribute to a life well-lived.

Almost six months to the day, on the morning of June 8, 2011, Elinor Esther Neumann Wilson, age 91, passed to her rest at the Elternhaus assisted-living facility. She had quietly supported and enthusiastically worked with her husband all over the world for 68 years. Besides her own skills as a wonderful Christian teacher, she will be remembered as the only woman to be the wife of a General Conference president and the mother of a General Conference president. She was buried quietly near her partner in life at the Ft. Lincoln Cemetery in Brentwood, Maryland.

More Interesting Facts

*It is interesting to note that Neal Wilson's 53 years of committed service (about two and a half more official years after his retirement and plenty more years of non-official service) were a duplicate of his father's service. One hundred and six years of service for Christ and the Church between father and son!

*The three Wilson ministers, father (Nathaniel), son (Neal), and grandson (Ted), all served on the General Conference Committee, the denomination's highest decision-making body. Each of the Wilsons also served as officers of the General Conference, and each has been president of a division of the world church, and two became president of the world church–a unique circumstance in Adventist history!

*The 58th General Conference Session (2005), in Saint Louis would be Elder Wilson's last General Conference session. His health would not permit him to attend the 59th session in Atlanta, Georgia, where his son would be elected president of the world church.

*Wilson presided over the first major restudy of Adventist beliefs in more than 50 years, culminating in the adoption of the 27 Fundamental Beliefs in 1980 at the Dallas General Conference session.

*As General Conference vice president for North America he emphasized full participation of African Americans in the life and work of the church. As president he continued to push for justice and equality.

*He confronted challenges to Adventist understanding of prophecy, the heavenly sanctuary, Ellen White's writings, the Sabbath; financial crises like the Davenport investments and the bankruptcy of Harris Pine Mills.

*He is as much at home in Africa, India, or South America as in the United States. He represented the church with dignity and grace as he met heads of state.

*In one of the final actions of his presidency, the General Conference session voted in a new division on July 5 (1990)-the Soviet Union.

Neal C. Wilson, 17th president of the General Conference

Neal Wilson's grandparents, Isabella and William Henry Wilson who joined the Adventist Church under Mrs. White's
preaching at a camp meeting in California in 1904.

(Left) Neal Wilson's parents, Nathaniel and Hannah Wilson in 1929
(Rightt) Nathaniel Wilson, father of Neal Wilson

(Left) Neal Wilson in 1934
(Right) Neal Wilson as a college student.

Nathaniel, Hannah, Neal and Clarice. Nathaniel is going overseas to be
Superintendent of the North Rhodesia Mission Field in 1925

Neal and Elinor Wilson

Wilson family in 1938

Elinor Wilson demonstrating her culinary skills

The four Wilson men: from left; Donald, Bruce, Nathaniel (father) , Neal.

Neal Wilson made racial integration a priority. Here he stands with the leaders of the
Columbia Union and the black Allegheny East Conference

Neal Wilson with a large group of clergy listening to President Ronald Reagan speak.
Picture courtesy of Pacific Press Publishing Association

Neal Wilson receiving his honorary Doctor of Divinity in 1976 at Andrews University

Neal C. Wilson and his wife, Elinor, enjoy the General Conference Parade of Nations with granddaughter Catherine.

Neal and Elinor enjoy the 54th World General Conference Parade of Nations in New Orleans after being reelected; granddaughter Catherine sits with them

Neal Wilson with the trustees of the White Estate

The group that climbed Mt. Kilimanjaro

Wilson meeting with President Bush and others

Neal Wilson greets a special guest from the Nepal embassy

Neal and Elinor at Christmas 2007, three years before his death.

Neal Wilson and Paul Harvey, news commentator

Elder Pierson passes the presidential torch to Elder Wilson

Leaving headquarters with Elder Bradford is Elder Maurice T. Battle (l.), Associate Secretary of the church's General Conference, Elder DeWitt S. Williams, president of the church's Central African Union.

EBONY • November, 1979

The North American Division became a separate entity while Wilson was serving. Charles E. Bradford became its first president. The story appeared in Ebony magazine. Bradford stands on the steps of the General Conference building with Maurice Battle, associate secretary and DeWitt Williams, president of the Central African Union.

Wilson traveled all over the world. Here he stands with leaders of Rwanda, Lance Butler, the treasurer of the General Conference, DeWitt Williams, president of Central African Union.

18. ROBERT STANLEY FOLKENBERG
July 6, 1990-February 8, 1999
(8 years)

Age When Elected President: 49 years old
Church Membership When Elected: 6.3 million members
Secretary: G. Ralph Thompson
Treasurer: Donald F. Gilbert

Born: January 1, 1941, in Santurce, Puerto Rico
Died: December 24, 2015, Winter Haven, FL. He was 74 years old.
Mother: Barbara Folkenberg, a teacher
Father: Stanley Folkenberg, a pastor, evangelist and church administrator
Siblings: Robert was oldest of three children-Don and Jeannie were also born in Puerto Rico
Wife: July 29, 1962, married Anita I. Emmerson
Children: Robert S., Jr. 1964
        Kathi Lynne, 1967
Ordained: December 24, 1966, Takoma Park, Maryland
Education: B.A and M.A. from Andrews University. Three honorary doctorates (D. D.); Southwestern (1990), Andrews (1991), and Atlantic Union College (1992).

Unexpected. Spanish-speaking. Multi-Talented.

Elder Folkenberg's election as president of the world church caught everybody by surprise and his exit from the office was equally unexpected.

Robert Folkenberg was born of missionary parents, Stanley and Barbara Folkenberg, in Puerto Rico on New Year's Day, 1941. His father was the first president of the Puerto Rico Mission. While living in Puerto Rico, Bob's brother, Don, and later his sister, Jeannie, were added to the family.

Bob's mother, Barbara, taught her children the first two grades, then Bob attended the third grade in the local church school. Bob's Spanish was doing fine but his English was so poor he went to Phoenix, Arizona, and lived with his maternal grandparents, Elder and Mrs. C. E. Andross (Elder Andross was the Arizona Conference President, and prior to that the president of the Caribbean Union). He also attended fourth grade in Phoenix Junior Academy and his English improved before returning to Puerto Rico.

After 10 years in Puerto Rico Bob's parents moved to Cuba where his father served in the Antillian Union. While in Cuba Bob took the fifth grade in a home school for missionary children in Havana. Then, in 1951, after 13 years in the Inter-American Division, his parents returned to the United States where his father served for nine years as district pastor and evangelist in Northern California. During these years Bob attended the church school in Yuba City, taking the sixth through the tenth grades. When his parents were called to pastor the Ukiah congregation Bob enrolled in Milo Academy for the last two years and graduated from Milo in 1958.

Bob's paternal grandfather, Louis E. Folkenberg, was the ninth child of Norwegian immigrants who homesteaded in the town of "Folkenberg" west of Portland, Oregon. His parents were the first Seventh-day Adventists in their family. Louis, also a pastor, cared for many congregations on the West Coast from Washington to California.

In 1958 Stanley Folkenberg was invited to join his brother, Elman, to lead out in the evangelistic program at the New York Center. Elman was the evangelist for the Atlantic Union where he and Dr. Wayne

McFarland developed the Five-Day Plan to Stop Smoking. After serving at the New York Center Stanley was called to be the evangelist for the New York Conference.

Bob attended Atlantic Union College for his first year of college. For his second year he broadened his global view by enrolling at Newbold College in England. Bob used his time at Newbold to develop his skills as a barber, something he had begun to learn during academy. Bob returned from Newbold to complete his Bachelor's and Master's degrees at Andrews University.

While at Andrews University Bob became acquainted with Anita Emmerson who was studying nursing at Loma Linda. Their long-distance courtship ended up in an engagement in December of 1961 and their wedding took place at the 1962 General Conference Session in San Francisco. Choosing the venue was a pragmatic decision since the Emmerson family friends were in Inter-America, North America and South America, and the Folkenberg friends were in Inter-America and North America. What better place for all to get together than at a GC Session!

Bob took flight training and financed it with his barbering. He carried a booklet in his pocket where he had the names of 200 regular clients. When he cut enough hair to fly an hour he would do so and continued until he got his private license in a Cessna 152. Upon concluding his studies Elder Nathaniel C. Wilson, president of the Michigan Conference, called Bob and Anita to begin their ministry in the Battle Creek Tabernacle. It was in Battle Creek that Bob, Jr. was born.

Folkenberg was called by the Columbia Union to join their evangelistic team, led by Roger Holley. It was during this period that Bob recorded his first album, used as a gift for attendees.

Meanwhile, Bob and Anita received a call to serve as pastor of a bi-lingual, ten-church district in Colon, Panama. After Elder Folkenberg's ordination, in December 1966, they began the long (10,000-mile) drive to Panama (via California to visit grandparents).

Caring for ten churches, where some spoke English and others spoke Spanish, was a challenge. Pastor Bob hadn't lived in a Spanish-environment for 15 years and his Spanish skills had degenerated. Fortunately, because much of Anita's education was in South America and her Spanish was fluent and accent-free, her copious note-taking was a huge help to Pastor Bob! It was while living in Colon that Kathi joined their family.

From Colon they moved to Panama City where Elder Folkenberg served as Conference evangelist and stewardship director. During this time Folkenberg built up hours by flying a plane for sky-divers on Sundays, took a course of aerobatics and built his flight time to the 200 hours which was required for a commercial license – the denomination's minimum requirement to do any church-related flying.

Bob's mother's side of the family also had some renowned ministers. Barbara's father, C. E. Andross, had been president of the Arizona Conference and president of the Caribbean Union. Barbara Folkenberg's great-great grandfather was Mills deForest Andross. He was born in Bradford, Vermont, in about 1805 and he died on March 6, 1836, in the Alamo. His son, William Henry Andross, moved from Vermont to Walla Walla, Washington, where he became the first Seventh-day Adventist in this family.

One of his sons, E. E. Andross, Barbara's grandfather, served in many positions in church leadership, including president of the Pacific Union (at the time the property for Loma Linda was purchased); president of the British Union; Vice President of the General Conference, and first President of the Inter-American Division. He also had the privilege of preaching the first funeral service for Ellen White (the one held in California before she was taken to Battle Creek).

Bob Folkenberg's wife, Anita, also came from a family of preachers and missionaries. Her father, Kenneth Harvey Emmerson, was the child of Harvey and Hazel McLean Emmerson. While attending PUC Kenneth Emmerson studied business and also met, fell in love with, and then married Dorothy Ayars, in 1938. Dorothy Ayars was born of missionary parents, also-Ernest and Irene Ayars. They were deeply involved with founding the college in Peru and Chile and served at the college in Argentina.

In 1970 Bob and Anita Folkenberg were called to move from Panama City to Tegucigalpa, Honduras, to serve as president of the Honduras Mission, a position he held until 1975. With both operating capital and liquidity more than 200% below zero the mission could not make payroll. Folkenberg invited a few businessmen to leave their businesses in the hands of their families and dedicate up to three years to planting a new church in an unentered area.

At the end of the period they had established more than 50 new congregations. Six of these laymen were offered and accepted employment as full-time pastors. Folkenberg was persuaded that medical work could be evangelistic. God led them to a village of "Valley of the Angels" about 20 miles from Tegucigalpa. The city fathers offered some land and an adjoining landowner offered some adjacent land at a very low price. Yet the mission didn't have any funding for the project. God blessed that initiative and He touched people's hearts. The hospital was built, equipped, staffed and four years later it was operating debt-free.

Though it has faced operational challenges over the years, the mission impact of this hospital resulted in the establishment of more than fifty congregations in that region. One of the challenges they faced in Honduras was transportation. The roads were so bad that on his first trip to the conference academy (8 hours and 125 miles away) drivers of heavy trucks ran him off the road twice.

It was evident to Bob now why God had planted in him an interest in flying. The Piper Super Cub which had been prepared for Elder Dick Hayden was offered to Bob, after Dick Hayden's untimely death. This plane was instrumental in establishing congregations in remote villages. Interestingly enough, on one trip to the northeast corner of Honduras, he found a submersible on the beach. Investigation proved it was a vehicle used to bring communist leaders to work with the Sandinista insurgents in Nicaragua.

After flying the Super Cub less than a year, a businessman offered to trade his four-seat Cessna 180 for it. Since it was a great bush plane, Folkenberg accepted the trade, did the maintenance required, named it after his great grandfather, E. E. Andross, and used the plane for 1000 hours. A later review of his flight logs indicated 70% of his landings (with all aircraft) were not in airports.

Then Folkenberg was called to serve as president of the Central American Union which included the seven countries from Belize to Panama. The much-longer distances demanded by the move to the Union required a faster aircraft. With the help of The Quiet Hour he traded the Cessna for a six-seat Piper Aztec. Though this was not as much of a bush plane he could still land on highways. They named it after pioneer missionary Orley Ford (who was also a distant relative of Bob's).

It became evident during an almost catastrophic experience flying to the US off the west coast of Mexico that, considering the type of flying he had to do, safety demanded a plane with weather-radar, turbo-charged engines, and oxygen in order to fly at higher altitudes. With the help of an Adventist businessman who owned an aircraft dealership he was able to trade the Aztec for a Navajo Chieftan.

During the five years (1975-1980) Folkenberg served as president of the Central American Union, his attention was focused on recovery from the magnitude 7.4 earthquake which struck central Guatemala on February 4, 1976. Thousands of people died that night. With the support of ADRA the Adventist Church in Central America was able to provide roofing for 10,000 homes as well as distribute many tons of humanitarian assistance to survivors, without regard to church affiliation – a factor that was acclaimed in the press.

Since the FAA requires that pilots get a bi-annual check ride (expensive but add little to one's skill-set) Bob chose, as often as possible, to get a new license instead. In this way he met the requirements of a biennial flight review while getting a new license with its new skill-set. Some of these new licenses included: an Instrument Rating, then an amphibious license (to fly a sea plane), and finally the "terminal degree" of flying, the Airline Transport Pilots Rating.

During the portion of a furlough spent with grandparents in California, Bob learned Pacific Union College had recently acquired a Bell G3B Helicopter. He was able to arrange for an instructor in Sacramento to give him lessons so during that furlough he was able to secure a commercial rating in a helicopter. While he rarely used a helicopter in Central America (the costs were too prohibitive to be practical), he did acquire a new skill-set.

During these years Bob recorded several more albums in English and Spanish since so little religious recorded music was available in Spanish.

At the General Conference Session in 1980 the Folkenbergs were called to serve at the Inter-American Division office in Miami. Immediately upon arriving in Miami it was evident that the cost of flying commercially was much less than flying privately. So, the Chieftan was sold and the proceeds were allocated to help pay for the cost of the short wave station in Costa Rica.

The years in the IAD office (1966 to 1985) were pleasant, challenging, and productive. Folkenberg helped to establish twelve more radio stations across the Inter-American Division.

In 1985 Elder A. C. McClure, president of the Southern Union, invited Folkenberg to serve as president of the Carolina Conference. They packed up again and moved to Charlotte, North Carolina. Folkenberg implemented a process to build funding and lay-ownership of church growth. The initiative, named "Carolina Breakthrough," was approved and is still in place almost 30 years later.

It was while they lived in Charlotte that Bob finally acquired another motorcycle. He had used a cycle during many of the years in Central America. They provided fast, low-cost transportation. He missed having one while in Miami and acquired a Honda Gold Wing. He frequently put his backpack into the trailer, drove into the mountains, and hiked to a quiet place in the mountains.

The General Conference Session in Indianapolis was one that the Folkenbergs would never forget. It began with Folkenberg's election as Nominating Committee Chairman. The first surprise was Neal C. Wilson not being voted in for another term as president. The next surprise was the Committee's first nomination for GC President, Elder George W. Brown, president of the Inter-American Division. Brown was the first non-white person to be nominated as president. Folkenberg and Brown had worked together for many years. As chairman Folkenberg had to inform Brown of the committee's recommendation. Folkenberg was dismayed when Elder Brown replied that he could not accept for personal reasons.

The committee started over and put names on the board. The next surprise came when Folkenberg's name was put on the board and he was asked to leave the room. Before he knew it, he was president of the General Conference of Seventh-day Adventists. The new president had spent 30 of his 49 years in Inter-America.

As president, Folkenberg led in reorganizing the General Conference Executive Committee and the representation system for delegates at the General Conference sessions. He promoted the Global Mission program energetically. He kept workers apprised of his activities by personally producing a computer-generated weekly newsletter. He was very computer savvy and bound the Adventist world together by improved technology and promoted satellite Net evangelistic series that went to a world audience.

Folkenberg believed in lay involvement and spent a great deal of his time raising money from private donors to operate church projects outside of the official denominational budget. It was this kind of involvement that proved to be his undoing.

James E. Moore, a Sacramento, California, entrepreneur, alleged that Folkenberg and other Adventist officials had cheated him and a charitable trust out of $8 million in promissory notes in a land deal in El Dorado County, California. Moore, who had been in bankruptcy and been convicted and imprisoned in 1989 for theft in an unrelated investment deal, taped several phone conversations with Folkenberg.

Moore finally filed a lawsuit against Folkenberg and several church entities. Leaders from all over the world flew into the world headquarters to decide what should be done and for several days in a sequestered location studied the situation. Finally, on Sunday, February 7, Folkenberg sent in a letter of resignation to G. Ralph Thompson who was now the acting president. On Monday, February 8, 1999, in a statement read before more than 600 employees at the world headquarters, Folkenberg stated that the distractions created by the lawsuit and the need for church unity made him realize it was best for him to resign. It was an emotional moment for the church that had learned to love Folkenberg and his church leadership for nearly nine years.

Fifteen years later, Folkenberg reminisced about the incident: "When a man I had known for more than twenty years sued me and the General Conference, the legal issues were resolved rather expeditiously. There were simply no transactions that involved the church or church assets in any way. I agreed it was a good idea for a church-appointed group to review the history. I sat in on the group to learn if I had done anything wrong, but soon they asked me to leave. I was disappointed since I had no idea what I had done wrong, if anything. Later, those who were present told me there was no misconduct on my part presented. There was plenty against this gentleman in his business transactions but those did not involve me or the church.

"While away from the meeting I concluded: 1) I was called to the ministry, not to any elected position, 2) As long as I remained in the presidency the focus would be on this litigation and would be a distraction from our mission. I realized I could resolve the entire issue rather quickly. So, I turned the car around and returned to the meeting room and submitted my resignation. Was it difficult? Yes, of course. Was it the right thing to do? Yes. So I did it."

More Interesting Facts

*Collectively, the Folkenberg and the Emmerson (Mrs. Folkenberg's side of family) families have given over 125 years of mission service to the Seventh-day Adventist Church in the Inter and South American Division as well as the Euro-Africa Division.

*After his resignation, Folkenberg had some time to think and pray about what he wanted to do for the rest of his life. The biggest problem he felt the church had was its low rate of growth in the economically-developed regions of the world. The wealthier the environment the slower the growth. A related factor in these same areas was a lower level of lay-ownership of mission compared to the economically less-developed parts of the world. So he started the ShareHim program.

The Carolina Conference sponsors the program. All contributions are received by the Carolina Conference and all operations are audited by the General Conference Auditing Service.

Using the Net 96 sermons as a starting point, Folkenberg spent a full year rewriting the "Truth For Today" sermons in English and translating them into Spanish. They were tested and a synchronization software developed so the speaker can see the notes on a laptop screen while the audience graphics are projected onto a screen. Then he developed a new "African" set in which explanations and pictures have an African context and another re-write for a Hindu audience. The sets are translated into more than 50 languages.

Later the programmer developed a proprietary software system (named "ShareSynch") that could use video clips with soundtracks and appeal songs. Since its inception in early 2001 ShareHim has enabled over 13,000 individuals (from 9 to 91 years of age) to preach a full, 19-sermon, campaign.

In January of 2005 ShareHim added a new, parallel, initiative which provides the resources free-of-charge to those who would like to lead out in Bible studies or experience evangelistic preaching in the "homeland."

Robert S. Folkenberg

Outgoing president Neal Wilson welcomes incoming president Robert S. Folkenberg

(Left) Pastor Stanley and Barbara Folkenberg, Robert (Bob) Folkenberg's parents.
(Right) Folkenberg's maternal grandfather, C. E. Andross, who at the time of this photo was president
of the Arizona Conference

(Left) Pastor Louis E. Folkenberg, the ninth child of Norwegian immigrants who homesteaded in the town of
Folkenberg, west of Portland, Oregon. Louis' parents were the first Adventists in the family.
(Right) Stanley and his brother Elman Folkenberg. Elman was the evangelist for the Atlantic Union where he and
Dr. Wayne McFarland developed the Five-Day Plan to Stop Smoking.

Young Bob with his brother Don and sister Jeannie who were all born in
Puerto Rico while their parents were missionaries there.

E. E. Andross and young Bob Folkenberg

The Folkenberg children a little older

Bob Folkenberg returning from Newbold College where he studied his second year of college.

Evangelist Stanley Folkenberg with a team member, Sunny Liu, the well-known tenor.

The wedding of Bob and Anita Folkenberg which took place at the 1962 General Conference Session in San Francisco.

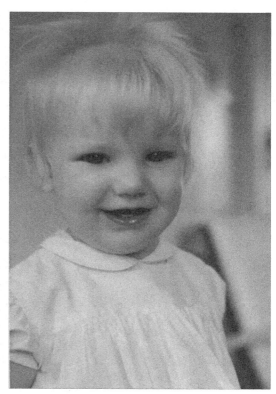

(Left) Bob, Jr. born in Battle Creek where Bob Folkenberg was pastoring.
(Right) Daughter Kathi Folkenberg born in Colon, Panama shortly afterward.

The Roger Holley Evangelistic team of the Columbia Union. Bob Folkenberg enjoyed full-time evangelism and being a singing evangelist. Folkenberg recorded his first album during this period which was used as a gift for attendees.

(Left) Bob and Anita Folkenberg in his office at the General Conference
(Right) Bob's mother celebrating her 90th birthday.

Bob Folkenberg stands next to his four-seat Cessna 180, a great bush plane, named after his great-grandfather, E. E. Andross.

Folkenberg standing beside a two-seat F-16. After a full day of training and fitting for the pressure flight-suit, the one hour flight accelerated from 0 to 175 mph in about four seconds. Flying at 500 mph it almost instantly went from level to straight up vertical. It took 24 hours in bed just to recover.

Son, Robert Folkenberg, Jr., making a point at the microphone. Photo: Gerry Chudleigh.

Folkenberg with his Honda Gold Wing motorcycle in Miami.
He usually rode it to the surrounding mountains for a quiet hike.

Bob Folkenberg on a camel in Israel.

The wedding of son Bob and Audrey Folkenberg Jr.

The wedding of grandchildren.

Pastor E. E. Andross, Barbara Folkenberg's grandfather, who served in many administrative positions, including vice president of the General Conference and president of the Pacific Union. He had the privilege of preaching the first funeral service for Ellen White (the one held in California before she was taken to Battle Creek).

There are many ministers and missionaries in the Folkenberg family. Bob's wife, Anita Folkenberg was born of missionary parents and grandparents. Her mother and father were Kenneth and Dorothy Ayars Emmerson. Anita's grandparents, Ernest and Irene Ayars were missionaries in South America and helped found the college in Peru. In the Ayars' family picture Dorothy is left on the back row and her daughter, Anita, (Bob's wife) is in the lap of Ernest Ayars, and her younger brother, Robert is in Irene Ayars' lap.

Kenneth Emmerson, Anita's father and former treasurer of the General Conference, was serving in Cuba when he became one of the few missionaries on active duty to be drafted to serve in the US military. He went ashore on D-Day plus 2 and served in the Allied headquarters in Paris. He remembered signing the payroll checks for Gen. Dwight Eisenhower.

Kenneth and Dorothy Ayars Emmerson.

(Right) George Brown, the president of the Inter-American Division, was the only non-Caucasian to be nominated as president of the General Conference. He declined and the vote went to Robert Folkenberg next who accepted.
(Left) While working in the Inter-American Division George Brown and Bob Folkenberg worked together. Here they are at the inauguration of the Central American Union Radio Station in Costa Rica while Elder G. W. Brown was the IAD President and Bob Folkenberg was his assistant.

19. JAN PAULSEN
March 1, 1999-June 23, 2010
(11 years)

Age when elected president: 64 years, 1 months
Church Membership When Elected: 10,939,182
Secretary: G. Ralph Thompson, Matthew A. Bediako
Treasurer: Robert L. Rawson, Robert E. Lemon

Born: January 5, 1935, in Narvik, Norway
Retired and living in Florida and Norway
Wife: Kari Trykkerud
Married: July 1, 1955
Children: Laila, 1961
              Jan-Rune, 1963
              Rein Andre, 1970
Mother: Alfhild Marie Konstanse Kristensen Paulsen
Father: Reidar Asløv Paulsen
Baptized: Age 14, August 1949, at a camp meeting in Melbu, north Norway by Pastor Frivold
Siblings: Older brother Roald, younger sisters Gerd and Inger
Ordained: 1963, in Accra, Ghana

Norwegian. Pastoral. Media.

Jan Paulsen was the second chief executive officer of the Seventh-day Adventist Church with Norwegian roots. The eighth president, Ole Olsen, was born in Norway but came to the United States when he was five years old. Elder Paulsen is also the second non-North American leader to be chosen as General Conference president. Charles Watson, the twelfth president, was from Australia. Paulsen was seen as a symbol of the increasingly non-American membership of the church. Ninety percent of the church's membership was outside of North America, with the most rapid growth occurring in the South Pacific, Africa, and South and Central America.

Paulsen came into office suddenly when Bob Folkenberg resigned. One of four children, he was born on January 5, 1935, in Narvik, Norway. He grew up in an Adventist home in Northern Norway where his father was a shoemaker. His mother was a soft-spoken, gentle person. Yet at the same time she possessed a deep, unwavering faith.

Mrs. Paulsen was baptized as a Seventh-day Adventist just a few months before Jan was born; his father and his uncles had already joined the church sometime before. Mrs. Paulsen's parents were evangelical Lutherans who belonged to a conservative group, the Laestadian movement, which still exists today, mostly in the northern parts of Norway, Finland, and Sweden. They were followers of a nineteenth century Swedish revivalist, Lars Levi Laestadius, whose emphasis on austerity and plain living led his followers to adopt strict religious practices.

In his grandfather's home there were no flower pots in the windows, no whistling, no wearing of neckties. When, as a child, Jan sat at the breakfast table he struggled to eat his porridge without sugar—a luxury forbidden by his grandfather. But when he had finished and had gone outside to his chores, his grandmother would say, "Now come . . .," and she would bring out the sugar. His grandfather's life was strongly driven by his religion, but Jan knew it was a form of religion he wanted no part of.

Jan's mother and grandmother preserved a warmth and a sweetness that seeped into the young child's life and they taught him to pray. His mother led him to sense the saving presence of Jesus Christ in his life.

Another person who profoundly shaped the course of Jan's life was his fifth-grade teacher, O. K. Naerland. He had traveled to the far north of Norway to help start a church school in his hometown of Narvik, teaching a dozen grade-school students in a one-room school adjacent to the church.

Jan was not a good student at that time. During the war years his family had evacuated to the country and his education had been erratic. Even after returning to Narvik he had not done well during the few months he spent in the local public school. In one subject especially—arithmetic—he had done very poorly. He had little self-confidence because he stuttered badly.

Yet under the care of this patient, kind teacher, something changed. The local school authorities kept up periodic checks on the little Adventist Church school to assure themselves that academic standards were high enough. During one visit by school inspectors, toward the end of the first year, Mr. Naerland gave him a math problem to solve on the chalkboard in front of the class. These inspectors knew well how poorly he had done in this subject in public school, and now they were amazed at the change! A year later he finished the seventh grade with the top mark in arithmetic in the town's schools.

Around this time young Paulsen also began to feel a strong attraction to the ministry. Some in the church said, "You, train for the ministry? With a stutter like that?" But Mr. Naerland encouraged and taught him not to accept limits that appeared to be overwhelming. He cared enough to recognize and develop the potential in his students. He taught young Jan what can be accomplished with proper attention, focus, and application.

Jan was baptized as a Seventh-day Adventist at age 14 and at age 15 he began to lay plans to enter the gospel ministry. After completing his early education in Narvik, he attended the Danish Junior College, Vejlefjord, where he majored in religion and did his ministerial internship training between 1952 and 1954.

Meanwhile, in the beautiful countryside of Southern Norway where winter sports are a part of daily life, a young lady by the name of Kari, the second of four children in her family, was facing some health challenges. She was born with a heart defect and when she was seven her parents were told that she would probably never grow up.

When she was eleven Kari was sent to Oslo, where there was a skilled cardiac surgeon who performed the complicated surgery. The surgery was successful, but secondary infection set in. Some American soldiers who happened to be patients at the same hospital heard about the child's struggle to survive and sent a wire to the states for penicillin which was not available in Norway at that time. The gift of penicillin cured her infection. Kari was touched by their kindness. She had been confirmed as a child in the state religion—Norway's Lutheran Church but she rarely attended.

At the age of thirteen she was given a Bible, her first, and found many confusing things in it as she read it. A year or two later, she met a church schoolteacher and his wife during a visit to her aunt, who was a Seventh-day Adventist. They gave her the book *Steps to Christ*. After much soul-searching, Kari was baptized in the Sauherad church and decided to attend an Adventist college.

Kari Trykkerud arrived two weeks late to the Adventist college in Denmark. The first class she attended was on the Old Testament prophets. The Danish numbering of the kings of Israel was totally different from the Norwegians. While she was trying to figure things out, confusion must have been written across her face. The young man sitting next to her leaned over and assured her, "Don't worry. I'll explain this counting thing afterward." This was the beginning of the relationship between Kari and Jan that would lead to their marriage later on July 1, 1955.

The first five weeks of their marriage were spent canvassing to earn a ticket to the United States where Jan was planning to continue his education. Young Paulsen went to America with thirty dollars in his pocket and nine months later they had earned enough money for Kari's ticket to join him at Emmanuel Missionary College (now Andrews University).

Young Paulsen was a scholar, earning a bachelor's degree before moving to Takoma Park, Maryland, where he earned a master's degree plus an additional year of graduate study at the Washington Theological Seminary.

The young couple went home to Norway where Elder Paulsen pastored for nearly two years before returning to Andrews University, bringing with them Laila, their first child born in 1961. Paulsen earned his Bachelor of Divinity degree while at Andrews.

Another teacher, a seminary professor, played a formative role in Elder Paulsen's life. Ted (Edward) Heppenstall was one of the leading Adventist theologians and teachers of his generation, whose influence is still felt in many ways in our church today. Paulsen first met Heppenstall and his wife, a Norwegian woman, when they visited Norway in the summer of 1955. He had just been appointed to teach at the seminary, then located in Washington, D.C. Paulsen was 20 years old and had plans to go to Emmanuel Missionary College to finish his last two years of college before moving on to the seminary. It happened that Heppenstall and Paulsen were both booked on the same boat from Oslo to New York City. During the time they spent together on the journey to America a bond developed that would continue during the years to come.

Heppenstall was a challenging, provocative teacher. He did not necessarily state things in the historic, traditional way. Paulsen remembers going to Heppenstall's office one day midway through the term and saying, "Dr. Heppenstall, you have destroyed everything I have believed about the sanctuary and you've given me nothing in place of it." Heppenstall replied, "Jan, remember—the sign of a mature mind is waiting until all the evidence is in." And he was right. As the term wore on, more concepts started to fit together. Heppenstall took his students down difficult paths of study—paths that are necessary for those who wish to function effectively as a minister. He did not shelter students from alternate ways of looking at things. He was profoundly loyal to the church and he would do his best to pull everything together into a structure that could be defended from the Bible. More than any other person, Dr. Hepenstall stimulated Jan Paulsen to search the Scriptures for himself.

Elder Paulsen stated in his own words the influence of these two on his spiritual life. "I see a certain symmetry between what I learned from my mother and what I received from Heppenstall. My mother helped me experience salvation. Ted Heppenstall helped me understand it. And there lies the bridge between faith and understanding that I believe is so important. If our faith is merely intellectual—even though we can explain it, defend it, even teach it to others—it is incomplete. We must also have the experience of faith, that sense of utter security that can come only from an uncomplicated trust in the goodness of God and in the sureness of His promises."

The Paulsens accepted a call to Ghana, where Jan was a Bible teacher at Bekwai Teacher Training College and pastor of the college church from 1962 to 1964. A son, Jan, was born there in 1963 and Paulsen was ordained to the gospel ministry there. They moved to the Adventist College of West Africa in Nigeria during 1964. Paulsen became head of the religion department, registrar and later president. Six months after their arrival in Nigeria the Biafran Civil War broke out.

Elder Paulsen was instrumental in setting up the first Adventist education degree program in sub-Saharan Africa while there. A call from Newbold College in England brought them back to Europe in 1968 where Paulsen became chair of the Department of Religion. Four years later Paulsen had earned a Doctor of Theology Degree from Tubingen University in Germany. Their third child, Rein-Andre, was born there.

Elder Paulsen and his expanded family returned to Newbold College and in 1976 he became president of the college. In 1980 he was elected secretary of the Northern European Division (now the Trans-European Division or TED). When division president Walter Scragg was called to the South Pacific in 1983, Paulsen was elected president of the TED.

St. Albans, England, became the home of the Paulsen family for the next fifteen years. During his Division presidency, Dr. Paulsen was influential in strengthening and expanding considerably the Adventist work in several countries of Eastern Europe after the collapse of communism, and assisted in establishing church organization in Albania which, until 1990, was closed to all religions. Elder Paulsen became a general vice president of the world church during the General Conference session in Utrecht, the Netherlands, in 1995 and the family moved to Silver Spring, Maryland.

Paulsen was first elected president at a special session of the church's executive Committee in March 1999, three weeks after Robert S. Folkenberg resigned from office. At the 57th world session held In Toronto, Canada, in 2000, Pastor Paulsen was unanimously reelected to a full five-year term as president.

In his Sabbath sermon Paulsen challenged the church. "It's late in the day; we're almost home; we cannot become reckless and careless. God chose us for a mission. We're not just one more sociological phenomenon-rather, God leads this church. Just like our Lord, our business is saving people. So, is your congregation able to communicate the atmosphere of warmth and loving acceptance?

"Size poses a challenge in terms of unity. We are not a fraternity [of different church organizations], we are one. I pledge to do all I can to make this church a place to be at home, a place to support each other-to carry each other if necessary-and to arrange our values and lives accordingly. Let us press together as we move forward to finish the journey." At this session the delegates also elected Matthew Bediako as General Conference Secretary. Elder Bediako, from Ghana, had been one of Paulsen's students.

As president, Paulsen initiated programs such as Go One Million, Faith and Science Dialogues, and Sow One Billion. As the Church entered the new millennium, Paulsen stood ready to give dynamic leadership to the rapidly growing church with its many challenging issues- mission, diversity, women's ordination, public perception of Adventists, quality of life for the world community, inclusion of youth and development of new leadership, to name a few.

Paulsen was the first president to make the most of visual media. His long-running *Let's Talk* television series, consisting of unedited, unscripted conversations with teenagers and young adults worldwide, helped the church embrace its younger generations. "Adventists About Life", a YouTube channel offered an Adventist perspective on current issues and opened the church to a more secular audience. The February 11, 2008, edition of *Night Talk* with Mike Schneider, a global cable network program of Bloomberg TV, featured President Paulsen in a one-hour interview. Paulsen sought opportunities to positively profile the Adventist Church. Adventist World and Hope Channel TV became global entities under his leadership.

More Interesting Facts

*Paulsen is the first president to hold an earned doctoral degree.

*He fluently speaks Norwegian, English, and German and also has a working knowledge of Hebrew, Greek, and Latin.

*In 1995 Andrews University presented Paulsen with a Doctor of Divinity degree (honoris causa) in recognition of meritorious service to the Adventist Church and excellence in Adventist education. He also received an honorary Doctor of Laws degree from Southwestern Adventist University, on May 5, 2001, and a Doctor of Divinity degree from La Sierra University, on June 17, 2001.

*Paulsen is the author of numerous articles and papers and of four books; *When the Spirit Descends, Let Your Light So Shine, Where Are We Going?* and *Let's Talk*.

*On November 11, 2011, Paulsen was named a Commander of the Royal Norwegian Order of Merit. This special award was presented by King Harald V of Norway at Tyrifjord Videregaende Skole on June 2, 2012.

Jan Paulsen

(Left) A youthful Kari and Jan with their children, baby Jan Rune and daughter Laila, on assignment in Ghana in 1963.
(Right) Kari and Jan Paulsen.

Paulsen at a meeting at Newbold College with some of his colleagues

Paulsen with mother, father, brother and sisters

Paulsen with his fifth grade class teacher, O. K. Naerland, and fellow students. Paulsen is in the back row, third from right.

The Paulsens flanked on the left by the Rawsons and on the right by the Bediakos.

On the TV program "Let's Talk Australia."

Paulsen in an interview with Bloomberg TV's Mike Schneider.

Jan Paulsen preaching at the Gangwashi Church, Bejing, during his historic visit to China, May 13-19, 2009. The visit was the first in decades by a Seventh-day Adventist world church president.

Richard Hart, Loma Linda University president, presents the institution's Presidential Medal to Paulsen during the worship service on January 23, 2010.

Paulsen receiving an honorary doctorate from Southwestern Adventist University.
Paulsen also received a D. D. from Andrews University in 1995.

Pastor Paulsen honored by Bishop Ole M. Chr. M. Kvarme (left) Church of Norway and OSCE High Commissioner on National Minorities Knut Vollebaek after receiving the Royal Norwegian Order of Merit at the Sabbath evening program during the East Norway Conference camp meeting June 2, 2012, at Tyrifjord Junior College.

Jan Paulsen, left, and Olsegun Obasanjo, former president of Nigeria and Babcock alumnus, at a Babcock University graduation ceremony, June 2009.

Elder Paulsen surrounded by happy children.

Elder Paulsen and the young people on the set of the Let's Talk TV program

During the opening meeting of the General Conference Session in Toronto, Canada, the general manager of *Canada Post*, Andre Ouelette, unveiled to Elder Paulsen the first Adventist stamp to be issued featuring the church.

Outgoing president and wife greet incoming president and wife.

Theologian and mentor Ted Heppenstall from Norway was one of the three people who had a profound influence on Jan Paulsen (the other two were his mother and fifth grade school teacher, O. K. Naerland).

On the first evening meeting of the 2000 Toronto session, President Paulsen took time to honor and pay tribute to the women and the children of the church, represented by his wife, Kari, for the women and Wesley and Stephanie for the children.

20. TED N. C. WILSON
June 23, 2010-

Age When Elected President: 60 years old
Worldwide Church Membership When Elected: 16,923,239
Secretary: G. T. Ng
Treasurer: Robert E. Lemon

Born: May 10, 1950, in Takoma Park, Maryland
Current General Conference president
Baptized: May 19, 1962, by his father Neal C. Wilson
Mother: Elinor Neumann, from Chicago, Illinois, a school teacher
Father: Neal Clayton Wilson, pastor and administrator and 17th president of the General Conference
Siblings: Shirley, born on January 24, 1953, in Cairo, Egypt
Wife: Nancy Vollmer, an occupational therapist. Married on September 14, 1975
Children: Emilie Louise Wilson DeVasher was born on July 11, 1978.
Elizabeth Esther Wilson Wright was born November 23, 1980.
Catherine Anne Wilson Renck was born January 4, 1983.
Ordained: July 8, 1978, at the Greater New York Conference camp meeting.
Education: B. A. Columbia Union College
MA and MPH joint program offered by Andrews and Loma Linda Universities
PhD. New York University

Informal. Supportive. Women's ordination.

Neal and Elinor Wilson had been in Egypt close to six years and were eligible to go home. Since Elinor was pregnant they requested their furlough.

Neal's sister, Ruth Murrill, was teaching nursing at Washington Sanitarium and Hospital in Takoma Park, Maryland, and it was decided that the "San" would be the best place for the delivery. Ruth and her husband Bill drove to New York to meet the soon-to-be parents who arrived by boat. Elinor had the baby almost as soon as they arrived, on May 10, 1950.

There was quite a bit of discussion about the baby's name. His paternal grandfather was Nathaniel Carter Wilson (N.C. Wilson) and his father was Neal Clayton Wilson (N.C. Wilson). Since Neal was not named after his father but had the initials N.C. in his name, it was decided that this pattern should be followed. Norman Clair Wilson (N.C. Wilson) finally surfaced. Ted's grandmother, Hannah Wilson, who had spent the last few years in Australia, thought that the new baby boy was cute and cuddly just like a Koala bear. In Australia they called those little bears Teddy and everybody started calling him Teddy. Nobody in the family ever called him Norman, just Teddy, and as he got older they got a little more sophisticated and called him Ted in public.

Elinor was her son's first teacher and she began reading to Teddy at an early age at home. About three years later the Wilsons would welcome another member of the family—a baby girl, Shirley who was born on January 24, 1953, in Cairo, Egypt.

When Neal Wilson was called to the Columbia Union, Ted attended Sligo school in Takoma Park, Maryland, for the last part of the fourth school year and finished his remaining elementary education (grades 5 to 8) at nearby John Nevins Andrews (JNA). The principal, Miriam Tymeson, exerted a strong influence on his life. Ted completed grades 9 to12 at neighboring Takoma Academy (TA).

Starting at an early age the Lord kept tugging at his heart. When he was twelve years old there were a series of special meetings at Takoma Park church. Elder E.L. Minchen made a very special and specific call for young men to come to the front to be ministers, to preach Christ, and young Ted responded to that call. Following that commitment, on May 12, 1962, his dad baptized him at the Takoma Park church.

Ted attended La Sierra College his first year then continued college at Columbia Union College. Ted graduated from CUC in April of 1970 at twenty years of age and went to New York for his internship at Patchogue. Patchogue was a small town on the south shore of Long Island named after the Native American tribe which once inhabited the area approximately sixty miles east of Manhattan. Ted enrolled in a joint program between Andrews University and Loma Linda University to earn a Master's of Divinity degree and a Master's of Science in Public Health. Greater New York Conference sponsored him at both places.

His first year at Andrews he worked in the business office and during his second year there Ted secured a job at WAUS, Andrews University's 24-hour classical radio station (90.7 FM) where he worked as a student announcer. He was on an hour program called *Morning Magazine* that delivered religious news, inspirational thoughts and music.

Ted first saw Nancy Vollmer at a friend's wedding in 1970 in a church in Takoma Park. Several years later Ted was in California attending the School of Public Health and saw Nancy at church sitting next to her grandmother, Mrs. Marion Vollmer. Ted and Nancy began dating and the romance blossomed. On September 14, 1975, they were married. Nancy Vollmer had been born into a prominent Adventist family. Her mother Mary Louise Evans Vollmer was the daughter of an Adventist preacher and administrator.

About 400 guests attended their wedding in Asheville, North Carolina, at Nancy's home church. The reception was held in the home Nancy grew up in. Elders Neal Wilson and Nathaniel Wilson performed the wedding ceremony.

Two years later Ted Wilson would serve as the assistant director and then director of Metro Ministry in New York City (October 1978). While serving as director of Metro Ministries Wilson was recommended for ordination, which took place July 8, 1978, at the Greater New York Conference camp meeting. Three days later Emilie Louise Wilson was born on July 11, 1978. Their second girl, Elizabeth Esther Wilson, would be born two years later, on November 23, 1980.

On September 21, 1981, Ted and Nancy and two little girls left New York City bound for Abidjan, Ivory Coast. They would work in a new division which brought together thirty countries and islands, home to approximately 250 million people, the majority of whom were French-speaking (officially named the Africa-Indian Ocean Division).

As ministerial association secretary, Wilson encouraged his pastors to evangelize and set an example by holding some meetings himself. Wilson pushed hard for a surge in evangelism during the One Thousand Days of Reaping (which set a goal to baptize 1000 new souls a day for 1000 days from September 18, 1982, to June 15, 1985, to add one million new members worldwide to the Church) and his zeal was infectious in AID. In 1985 Wilson was elected secretary of the division but he still promoted evangelism in AID and the Harvest '90 program.

Their last daughter, Catherine, was born during the time they were in Africa but Nancy flew back to the States and Catherine was born in Asheville, North Carolina.

A few years later Ted Wilson was ready to tackle another big project–climbing Mount Kilimanjaro. Neal Wilson spent 25 years in Africa-10 years as a boy and 15 as a missionary in Egypt. He had climbed many mountains in Africa and had always entertained the hope of one day climbing Mount Kilimanjaro but he never seemed to have the time or the opportunity.

Ted Wilson, realizing that the 1988 Annual Council would be held in Nairobi, Kenya, saw an excellent opportunity for his father to realize this dream. Since he was the secretary of the division and already lived in the Ivory Coast and knew many of the leaders there he began to lay careful plans for his father to climb the 19,340 ft. mountain just before the session. Mount Kilimanjaro, the highest point on the continent of Africa, was just south of the Annual Council meeting place in Arusha, Tanzania.

On September 12-16, six Seventh-day Adventists, including a father and son, two laypeople, two editors (William Johnsson and Delbert Baker), began that climb hoping to succeed. Every year about 5000 people came from around the world to climb to the summit. On average, one in four reached the top. But all six Adventists were successful.

The Wilsons had intended to stay in Africa for another three years but when they returned to attend the General Conference session in 1990 Ted was asked to be an associate secretary of the General Conference. He accepted and the family moved to Maryland. In this new position he was in charge of overseeing the Africa-Indian Ocean Division, the same division he had served in, as well as being the liaison with SUD, the Southern Asian Division and EUD. While he was serving in this post at the General Conference he received a request to go as president to ESD, the former Soviet Division. He studied Russian at the Silver Spring headquarters and the family soon left for Moscow.

Robert Kinney who had been voted in as the 16th president at a specially called meeting of the Review and Herald board indicated his desire to retire. The board met quickly and elected Ted N. C. Wilson, who had just returned from Russia, as the 17th president of the Adventist Church's oldest and largest publishing house.

In the November 6, 1996, year-end meeting Ted N. C. Wilson and Bob Kyte, president of the Pacific Press Publishing Association presented the current challenge of the trend of declining subscriptions to magazines published by the two houses. In his overhead presentation Wilson and Kyte solicited suggestions from the group as to how they could meet this challenge. Some magazines would be merged and some would be eliminated. Appreciation was expressed to presidents of both publishing houses for the production of Net 96 materials.

The 59th General Conference Session held in Atlanta, Georgia, in 2010 elected Ted Wilson as the world church president. After the session concluded, Wilson returned to Silver Spring, Maryland, and moved into the president's office about 40 feet down the hall from his previous office.

Elder Wilson describes his leadership style: "I like to be rather informal. I like to get participation. I like to hear people's views. I like to come to a consensus. I believe in servant leadership. I like for people to feel that I'm accessible and that other leaders are accessible. I like to have a balanced approach in which we listen carefully to people, we are fair with people, and we don't brush people off. Leadership involves a lot of listening, a lot of praying, and then careful analysis and asking the Lord to guide us in the right way. And if we make a mistake, we shouldn't be too proud to say, 'Well, maybe we ought to try this way.' You need to be flexible and open, and in the long run, to realize that leadership really is to depend wholly on the Lord. I absolutely believe that. He will not leave us without direction. This is the object of His supreme regard-this precious Church-and I have every confidence that God will give us the answers to the challenges we face."

Ted N. C. Wilson is quick to tackle big jobs and doesn't mind working unseen and silently behind the scenes. Shortly after being elected, he presented one of his favorite projects to the workers by challenging them to distribute Ellen White's book *The Great Controversy* to every household in the postal area surrounding the headquarters. In closing comments before a dedicatory prayer for the project, Wilson pointed to the positive impact of the distribution project: "Those who are truly seeking truth will be attracted to this book," he said. "Additionally, the project will serve as encouragement for church administrative offices and individual churches worldwide to participate in similar distributions."

The response to his vision and to the book project was overwhelming. Employees donated more than $50,000 – approximately 42 percent more than was needed – to fund the printing and mailing of *The Great Controversy*, to the 22,000 homes in the 20904 zip code (Silver Spring, Maryland) in which the headquarters building was located. Money raised above the basic costs would go toward sending copies of the book to the adjacent geographical areas.

Each copy of *The Great Controversy* includes an invitation card for a Bible correspondence course, an unobtrusive way to encourage Bible study. After challenging the workers at the General Conference, President Wilson challenged the world fields to undertake a massive worldwide distribution of the book.

Wilson's next step was to bring his vision of revival and reformation to the leaders and representatives of the Adventist Church assembled at the world headquarters for the October 2010 Annual Council. The main item on the agenda was revival and reformation. Delegates shared how God had impacted their lives and how they longed to see Christ's return. They prayed together and asked for an outpouring of the Holy Spirit and then voted an amazing document called "God's Promised Gift: An Urgent Appeal for Revival, Reformation, Discipleship, and Evangelism."

He next challenged the delegates assembled at the 2011 Annual Council to adopt a sustained, comprehensive urban evangelistic outreach called Mission to the Cities. The goal was to reach approximately 650 major cities of the world before the next General Conference Session in 2015, all based on the power of the Holy Spirit through revival and reformation. He asked members all over the world to pray at 7:00 in the morning, 7:00 in the evening for seven days of the week. The 777 prayer initiative should focus attention on the incredible Mission to the Cities.

A big question remained unanswered during the first five years of Wilson's administration. *Should the Adventist Church ordain women to the gospel ministry?* Several meetings had been tasked to answer this divisive question and some local conferences had moved ahead independently and ordained women.

Some members claimed that the Bible, and especially Paul, shows a male priesthood which is still the model for today. Others claim that since the church is made up of a large percentage of qualified women who share a burden to proclaim the gospel in these modern times, women must be ordained in order to finish the work. God has promised to pour out His Spirit on *all* flesh, which must include women. China is given as an excellent example.

Wilson promised to adhere to whatever decision the 60th General Conference session made on women's ordination. Some faulted Wilson because he did not promote his position and lead the Church in this area but assigned the question to committees.

Wilson did not want his personal opinion to dominate the answer to this question. He asked each delegate to consider this statement: "After your prayerful study on ordination from the Bible, the writings of Ellen G. White, and the reports of the study commissions, and, after your careful consideration of what is best for the church and the fulfillment of its mission, is it acceptable for division executive committees, as they may deem it appropriate in their territories, to make provision for the ordination of women to the gospel ministry? Yes or No."

The answer came on Wednesday, July 8, 2015. During the Wednesday afternoon session, dozens of people took turns at microphones to state their views in two-minute speeches before lining up to write their votes on a secret ballot that was placed in one of five clear boxes at the front of the assembly hall in San Antonio's Alamodome and Convention Center. The vote, 1381 against to 977 in favor, was expected by some since the majority of the membership is outside of North America and is much more conservative. Some who might have voted in favor of women's ordination also voted against the proposition since they wanted the Church to move in a united way rather than each region separately. After the vote Wilson challenged the members to stay united and to remember the Biblical and Spirit of Prophecy mission placed upon the Church.

More Interesting Facts

*Ted Wilson attended New York University for his doctoral studies. The title of his dissertation was "A Study of Ellen G. White's Theory of Urban Religious Work as It Relates to Seventh-day Adventist Work in New York City". The dissertation was "Submitted in partial fulfillment of the requirements for the degree of Doctor of Philosophy in the School of Education, Health Nursing, and Art Professions, New York University, 1981."

*On November 3, 2009, after the required posting, by order of the Circuit Court for Montgomery County, Domestic System, "Ted" was added officially to his name. His family and friends had called him Ted so long that no one really knew him as Norman (Norman Clair Wilson). For legal and personal reasons he would now officially be Ted N. C. Wilson.

(Some of this information came from *Highly Committed, The Captivating Story of the Wilson Family and Their Impact on the Adventist Church*, DeWitt S. Williams, 2013, Teach Services, www.teachservices.com).

Father and son- Neal and Ted Wilson

Ted N. C. Wilson

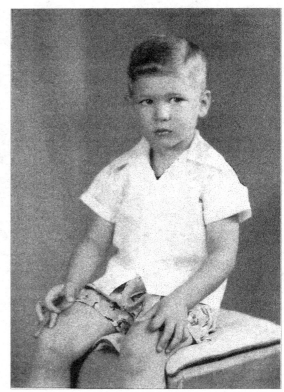

(Left) Neal and Elinor Wilson with their children, Ted and Shirley, 1953.
(Right) Ted Wilson at 3 years of age

Ted and Nancy with daughters Emilie, three years old and Elizabeth, two months old in 1981.

Emilie Wilson being escorted down the aisle by her father at her wedding

President Ted Wilson with wife Nancy

The Ted Wilson family with daughters, sons-in-law and grandchildren. Photo: Gina Wahlen.

The Ted Wilson family increasing

The Wilsons visit India.

Wilson and other leaders promote the *Great Hope*/*Great Controversy* project.

Advent Hill Primary School, Nairobi, Kenya, Pathfinder Club, April 23, 2011. Edward Onyango photo.

The Triadelphia, Maryland church quartet. From left: first tenor, James Shroader; second tenor, Bill Fagal; baritone, Ted Wilson; bass, Gaspar Colon.

The Thailand welcoming committee.

Wilson wearing national dress.

Wilson at the centennial celebration of Spicer Memorial College

Wilson in Japan.

Wilson baptizes a Vietnamese candidate.

Nancy Wilson with Elaine Oliver at Neal C. Wilson's funeral.

Wilson emphasizing his program to the cities.

The Wilsons in Vietnam.

Wilson's team of nine Vice Presidents during his first term.

The secretarial team at the GC 2014

SECRETARIES OF THE GENERAL CONFERENCE OF SEVENTH-DAY ADVENTISTS

—ɷ—

1. Uriah Smith 1863-1873
2. Sidney Brownsberger...............1873-1874
3. Uriah Smith..............................1874-1876
4. Charles W. Stone.....................1876-1877
5. Uriah Smith..............................1877-1881
6. Adolph B. Oyen 1881-1883
7. Uriah Smith..............................1883-1888
8. Dan T. Jones............................1888-1891
9. Willard A. Colcord..................1891-1893
10. Leroy T. Nicola 1893-1897
11. Lewis A. Hoopes....................1897-1901
12. Howard E. Osborne...............1901-1903

13. William A. Spicer...................1903-1922
14. Arthur G. Daniells..................1922-1926
15. Cecil K. Meyers 1926-1933
16. Milton Earl Kern....................1933-1936
17. Ernest D. Dick.......................1936-1952
18. Denton E. Rebok....................1952-1954
19. Walter R. Beach 1954-1970
20. Clyde O. Franz.......................1970-1980
21. G. Ralph Thompson...............1980-2000
22. Matthew A. Bediako 2000-2010
23. G. T. Ng.................................2010-

A BRIEF HISTORY OF THE SECRETARIAT

The Secretariat of the General Conference was inaugurated at the same time the General Conference itself was established. On May 20, 1863, the "Constitution of the General Conference" was approved by the 20 delegates, and among other items, stated that there "shall be a President, Secretary, Treasurer and an Executive Committee of three." The specific tasks of the Secretary were not delineated.

In the first forty years of the church's existence, the Secretary featured prominently in its governance. His views carried great weight with other church leaders in debates and discussions. Every major decision taken by General Conference Sessions or the GC Executive Committee was summarized and recorded by the Secretary.

These included rulings on church organization; missionary strategy and placement; creation of new church entities; and decisions on policy, doctrine, financial matters, and the denominational stance on political and governmental matters. The Secretary played a negotiating role between potential antagonistic parties, brokering agreements, drafting official documents, and dealing with dissident groups. Most of the early records were recorded right in the *Adventist Review* for the entire church to see and read. Until 1889, all terms of office were for one year (more or less). Today, the second officer of the Adventist Church is usually called the Executive Secretary.

1. Uriah Smith
May 20, 1863-November 14, 1873
(Ten years)

Age when elected Secretary: First time- 31 years old
Local Conferences and Missions: 6
Ordained Ministers: 22
Churches: 125

Born: May 2, 1832, in West Wilton, New Hampshire
Died: March 6, 1903, in Battle Creek, Michigan. He was 70 years old.

Inventor. Writer. Editor. Teacher. Poet. Artist. Preacher. Administrator. Uriah's family became Millerite Adventists so at age twelve he experienced the 1844 Disappointment. Also at age twelve his left leg had to be amputated as a result of an infection. Annie Smith was his talented older sister who had 45 of her poems appear in the *Review and Herald* and *Youth's Instructor*.

After the Disappointment Uriah became disinterested in religion for a while and pursued education. He attended Phillips Academy in Exeter, New Hampshire. When his sister, Annie, accepted the seventh day Sabbath in 1852, Uriah accepted it also. James White recognized Uriah Smith's talent of writing and invited him to assist in the publication of the *Review*.

The father of the family was Samuel Smith and his wife, Rebekah Spalding Smith. Samuel was a man of ability and at one time of wealth. He was a highway builder and contractor, and his mechanical genius was seen also in his sons. In his later years he suffered financial losses which were the reason Uriah was not able to pursue his ambition to enter Harvard University. Mrs. Smith was a lady of culture and some of her poems appeared from time to time in the *Review*.

In June, 1857, Uriah married Harriet Stevens, a sister of J. N. Andrews' wife, Angeline. Harriet was known for her hospitality and charitable deeds. The Smiths had five children–four boys and one girl.

For fifty years Uriah Smith had a close connection with the church paper, most of the time as editor-in-chief. When the first General Conference was organized he was elected its first secretary. He held the position of secretary four separate times for a total of twenty-two years. From 1876 to 1877 he also served as General Conference treasurer.

Smith was ordained to the gospel ministry in 1874. When Battle Creek College was founded in 1874, Elder Smith became the first Bible teacher, a position he held for the next eight years.

An artist as well as a writer, Uriah Smith produced many of the first illustrations that appeared in the *Review*. He was a prolific writer producing many articles and books. His most famous book was *Thoughts on Daniel and the Revelation*. He wrote some 4,000 editorials and authored twenty books.

After his leg was amputated he invented and patented an artificial leg with a movable ankle and with the money received from its sale he bought his first house in Battle Creek. He patented other inventions such as a school desk with an improved folding seat. Uriah always walked with a cane and would limp down Washington Street bound for his editorial office at the Review and Herald building which burned two months before his death. Uriah Smith remains the most versatile of the Adventist pioneers.

2. Sidney Brownsberger
November 14, 1873-August 10, 1874
(One year)

Age when elected Secretary: 28 years old
Local Conferences and Missions: 14
Ordained Ministers: 51
Churches: 239

Born: September 20, 1845, in Perrysburg, Ohio
Died: August 13, 1930, in Fletcher, North Carolina. He was 84 years old.

Sidney grew up on the family farm. While a student at the University of Michigan, Ann Arbor, he heard of the beliefs of Adventists. He purchased all of the Adventist literature printed at that time. During his busy student life he spent much time in Bible study and in reading these books. Without ever having seen a Seventh-day Adventist he began keeping the Sabbath alone during his junior year in college in 1868.

When he graduated he became superintendent of public schools in Maumee, Ohio. At the request of Elder and Mrs. White in 1873 he accepted the call to help establish Battle Creek College, the first educational institution of the denomination. While there he taught and also served for a year as secretary of the General Conference. He served as the first principal of Battle Creek College from 1874 to 1881. He married Florinda Camp and they had three children: John, Berdena and Daisy. In 1875 he received his M. A. from the University of Michigan.

A demand for a college on the Pacific Coast called Professor Brownsberger from Battle Creek to establish Healdsburg College, today known as Pacific Union College. He stayed there for five years. In 1909 Professor Brownsberger shared in the establishment of the Asheville Agricultural School and Mountain Sanitarium. Sidney Brownsberger was very well educated for his day. Besides being Secretary of the General Conference, he made significant contributions to the Seventh-day Adventist Church as first president of two colleges, cofounder of a medical institution and school, and initiator of the first business and health curricula in an Adventist college.

3. Uriah Smith
August 10, 1874–September 19, 1876
(Two years)

Age when elected Secretary (Second Time): 42 years old
Local Conferences and Missions: 16
Ordained Ministers: 60
Churches: 300

See #1 for his bio.

4. Charles Wesley Stone
(September 19, 1876-September 20, 1877)
(One year)

Age when elected Secretary: 28 years old
Local Conferences and Missions: 16
Ordained Ministers: 96
Churches: 398

Born: 1848, in Vermont
Died: July 27, 1883, in Carlton, New York (Killed in a train accident). He was 35 years old.

Charles Stone was the son of Albert and Lovina Stone. He grew up in Vermont and in 1868 married a Vermont girl, Inis Purinton, not yet an Adventist. She was converted to Adventism soon after her marriage and was a great support to her husband.

Stone was a Vermont delegate to the General Conference session of 1876 and at that time was elected secretary of the General Conference, auditor of the Review and Herald Publishing Association, and local editor of the *Advent Review and Sabbath Herald*. In 1879 he was ordained to the ministry and was called to Battle Creek College, where he served as principal of the business department and also taught singing (which he had studied in Boston and New York). Stone helped compile the songbook *Better Than Pearls* published 1881.

In 1883 he was teaching public schools in Battle Creek when he wrote *Captain of Our Salvation*. On July 27, 1883, while he and his wife were traveling on the railroad in New York his train, traveling at a high speed, crashed into an overturned freight car. Nineteen people were killed outright, including Elder Stone.

His wife suffered a broken arm and several other injuries. Stone was just thirty-five years old. In the funeral notice General Conference President G. I. Butler noted that he had been an outstanding public speaker and perhaps the most musically gifted of the Adventist ministers at that time. Inis Stone, still a young woman at the time of his death, later married Dr. James Osborne of Missouri and died on March 7, 1919.

5. Uriah Smith
September 20, 1877-December 1, 1881
(Four years)

Age when elected Secretary (Third Time): 45 years old
Local Conferences and Missions: 18
Ordained Ministers: 106
Churches: 478

See #1 for his bio.

6. Adolph Bernard Oyen
December 1, 1881-November 8, 1883
(Two one year terms)

Age when elected Secretary: 24 years old
Local Conferences and Missions: 31
Ordained Ministers: 148
Churches: 640

Born: April 15, 1857, in Troudbjem, Norway
Died: March 24, 1940, in Chicago, Illinois. He was 82 old.

Adolph was born in Norway to Frederick and Anna Oyen. He immigrated to the United States in 1861 and later became an Adventist and also married Jennie Sprague. They had three children: Albert, Winifred and Shirley May.

Oyen was a teacher on the first faculty of Battle Creek College where he taught Danish. He later served as an editor of the *Youth's Instructor* in 1883 while at the same time was secretary of the General Conference (1881-1883).

Oyen went as a missionary to Scandinavia with E. G. Olsen in 1884 to supervise the publishing work and build up the Scandinavian mission. From October 30 through November 2, 1885, Ellen White lived in his home while she visited Adventists in Norway. She appreciated being able to converse with Elder Oyen in English and he served as Sister White's interpreter.

Oyen married May V. Johnson in 1914 who was thirty years younger than he was. Sister White did not approve of this.

7. Uriah Smith
November 8, 1883-October 17, 1888
(Five years)

Age when elected secretary (Fourth Time): 51 years old
Local Conferences and Missions: 29
Ordained Ministers: 165
Churches: 680

See #1 for his bio

8. Dan T. Jones
October 17, 1888-March 5, 1891
(Three years)

Age when elected secretary: 33 years old
Local Conferences and Missions: 39
Ordained Ministers: 232
Churches: 901

Born: March 25, 1855, in Kingsville, Missouri
Died: September 24, 1901, in Kingsville, Missouri. He was 46 years old.

Dan Jones became an Adventist in 1876 at age twenty-one. He became very active in the church and in 1881 was ordained to the gospel ministry. The next year he was elected president of the Missouri Conference. He was so effective that he was soon called by the General Conference to serve on the General Conference Committee and other boards and in 1888 as Secretary of the General Conference. In 1889 he served on the committee that prepared the constitution of the National Religious Liberty Association.

He was married to Clara E. Low on August 28, 1888. When he moved to Battle Creek, Michigan, he worked so hard that his health began to fail. He moved West hoping that his bronchitis would improve. The doctors informed him that he would have to have absolute rest and retirement in the drier climate of Colorado.

After a period of rest, under the advice of Dr. Kellogg he went with his family to Guadalajara, Mexico, to open up medical missionary work among the Spanish-speaking people of that country. He went with several teachers and medical personnel. He spent nearly eight years of continuous labor in Mexico under great difficulties but the Guadalajara Sanitarium stands as a tribute to his pioneering efforts. His baby girl, Carmen, died in Guadalajara.

Elder Jones had the satisfaction of seeing the work permanently established in Mexico and Guadalajara Sanitarium operating on a good financial basis. He learned that he had Bright's disease and he soon passed away at age forty-seven. His wife Clara and his daughter Edna returned to Mexico to continue the work there. Clara became secretary of the Sabbath school department of the Mexican Mission. Less than five years later she passed away at age 46.

9. Willard Allan Colcord
March 5, 1891-March 8, 1893
(Two years)

Age when elected secretary: 30 years old
Local Conferences and Missions: 42
Ordained Ministers: 230
Churches: 1066

Born: December 8, 1860, in Coleta, Illinois
Died: November 4, 1935, in Washington D.C. He was 74 years old.

Willard was the son of Ivory G. and Charlotte Colcord who had seven children. His early life was spent in Coleta where he also obtained his education. When he was about twenty-four he became an Adventist and joined the church in Grand Junction, Iowa.

Willard then received further education at Battle Creek College and pastored in Iowa from 1886 to 1888. Then he engaged in editorial work for the General Conference from 1888 to 1893. For two years during this period he served as secretary of the General Conference. He then went to Australia for editorial and administrative work for the Bible Echo Publishing House from 1893 to 1902.

In 1898 he was invited to join Ellen White's literary staff in Australia. When he returned to the United States he taught for two years at Union College (1902-1904). Then he became associate secretary in the GC Religious Liberty Department (1904-1910) and was also on the book committee of the Review and Herald Publishing Association (1907-1914).

Not long after this he lost his faith in the distinctive doctrines and leadership of the Adventist Church and for twenty years he did not attend church. In January 1934 he released a statement that was published in the *Review and Herald* confessing his error and was rebaptized into the fellowship of the church. He died in 1935 with full confidence and trust in Christ and the Adventist message. He and his wife, Anna L. Colcord, had two sons, Clarence and Glenn, and one daughter.

10. Leroy Thomas Nicola
March 7, 1893-February 19, 1897
(Four years)

Age when elected secretary: 37 years old
Local Conferences and Missions: 46
Ordained Ministers: 267
Churches: 1151

Born: February 21, 1856, in Pilotsburg, Iowa
Died: January 2, 1940, in Battle Creek, Michigan. He was 83 years old.

Leroy Thomas Nicola was baptized at the age of eighteen and in 1874 entered Battle Creek College during its inaugural year. He interrupted his studies because of an urgent need of pastors in Iowa but returned and graduated in 1880. He resumed the ministry in 1881 and in that same year married Sylvia Hillis whom he had met at Battle Creek College. Five years later he was ordained to the gospel ministry. He engaged in pastoral ministry in Des Moines, Iowa, for twelve years, returning to Battle Creek in 1893 to serve as secretary of the General Conference. In 1898 he was placed in charge of the International Tract Society of New York City and served as a pastor in New York, Massachusetts, and Michigan.

During his pastorate in Lansing, Michigan, Mrs. Nicola died in 1918. He returned to Battle Creek to care for his aging father and mother. He loved to visit the members of his church and was often on his knees in prayer with them. He took a great interest in Oak Hill Cemetery where many of the Adventist pioneers were buried. It was his custom to take visitors to Battle Creek and guide them as he pointed out the resting places of the pioneers. He also preserved a number of Adventist historical items of significant value to the church.

He had two sons, Forrest and Howard, and two daughters, Nelly and Mary. He died on January 2, 1940, and is buried in his beloved Oak Hill Cemetery.

11. Lewis Azariah Hoopes
February 19, 1897-April 2, 1901
(Four years)

Age when elected secretary: 37 years old
Local Conferences and Missions: 61
Ordained Ministers: 407
Churches: 1574

Born: April 20, 1859, at Westlane, Ohio
Died: May 14, 1925, in Hinsdale, Illinois. He was 66 years old.

Lewis was the son of Isaac and Mercy King Hoopes. He and his twin sister, Mercy Maria, were born in 1859. Lewis spent his early life in agricultural pursuits but was educated at the State University of Nebraska at Lincoln. While he was teaching at this university he was converted and accepted the Sabbath in 1882. He was baptized in 1883 and began immediately to sell denominational literature and do evangelistic work. He was married on September 4, 1883, to Emma A. Snyder.

Elder Hoopes was ordained to the gospel ministry in 1885 and in 1889, at the young age of thirty, he was elected president of the Nebraska Conference. He assisted in the founding of Union College when he was called there to be the Bible instructor. For some time Hoopes served as coeditor of *Christian Record*, a braille magazine for the blind.

Elder Hoopes was then called to the General Conference to be the secretary for four years. Thereafter he was president of Union College for four years and then left to go to Australia to assist in the development of the educational work there. After nine years in Australia he returned to America and connected with Graysville Academy in Tennessee as a Bible teacher. From Tennessee he went to Nevada, Iowa, where he was principal and Bible teacher at Oak Park Academy for several years.

In 1920 he and Emma moved to Hinsdale, Illinois, where Elder Hoopes served as chaplain of the Hinsdale Sanitarium until his death on May 14, 1925. He was buried in the Hinsdale Cemetery. The

Hoopes had one son, Samuel. Their oldest daughter, Ethel, would marry another minister who would become the secretary of the General Conference, C. K. Meyers. The other two daughters, Mildred and Vera, would marry into the Watts family and would serve as missionaries. Emma Hoopes survived her husband by twenty-four years and died on July 18, 1949, in California. Elder Dwight Nelson, pastor of the Pioneer Memorial church at Andrews University, is his great-great grandson.

12. Howard Edgerly Osborne
April 2, 1901-April 11, 1903
(Two years)

Age when elected secretary: 27 years old
Local Conferences and Missions: 98
Ordained Ministers: 553
Churches: 2011

Born: September 13, 1873, in Hartland, Maine
Died: February 24, 1908, in San Pasqual, California. He was 34 years old.

Howard was the son of Elder Peter B. Osborne who was a veteran of the Civil War and for many years a Seventh-day Adventist minister in Maine. Howard attended South Lancaster Academy for four years and Battle Creek College for two years after which he spent several years in the religious liberty work in the ministry in the states of New York and Maine.

He was elected General Conference Secretary in 1901 but a severe attack of pleuropneumonia led him to resign his secretarial post and move to California for his health. The change in climate restored his health. There he married Jesse Barber, on December 21, 1904. From 1905 to 1906 he taught English at Healdsburg College (now PUC) and from 1906 to 1908 at San Fernando Academy. His health again failed here in the warm climate. After only four years of marriage he died of typhoid fever at age thirty-four.

At the time of his death they had a little one-year-old daughter, Barbara. Sister Osborne traveled to Maine with her little daughter where she made her home with her husband's parents. She taught at South Lancaster Academy. In 1915 she moved back to California and connected with Pacific Union College and made her home there for forty-two years as an outstanding teacher. In 1927 she bravely and cheerfully saw her only daughter, now Mrs. Henry Westphal, go to South America as a missionary. In 1957 she went to Miami, Florida, to live with her daughter who had returned from mission service. Jesse Osborne died on September 9, 1959, and was buried in San Pasqual, California, beside her husband who had died fifty-one years earlier.

13. William Ambrose Spicer
April 11 1903-May 11, 1922
(Nineteen years)

Age when elected secretary: 37 years old
Local Conferences and Missions: 126
Ordained Ministers: 616
Churches: 2120

Born: December 19, 1865, in Freeborn, Minnesota
Died: October 17, 1952, in Takoma Park, Maryland. He was 86 years old.

With the reorganization of the church governance structure from 1901 to 1903, the office of Secretary underwent an expansion. In one way the Secretary's duties were lessened for, with new organizational structures like unions, the herculean task of church governance was parceled out, with responsibilities shared with other levels of denominational authority.

However, the Secretary's responsibilities were actually increased, because, with more sophisticated governing structures, increasing membership, and expanding missions, ultimately there was more for the General Conference to oversee. A Statistical Secretary was appointed, working under the Secretary. In 1901 the General Conference Executive Committee took responsibility for foreign mission work from the Foreign Mission Board which had not functioned effectively. The Secretary became responsible for the General Conference's missions operations for the worldwide mission enterprise of the Seventh-day Adventist Church as a whole.

At the close of the reorganization period, one of the most important Secretaries in the history of the church was appointed. William Ambrose Spicer revolutionized the position, molding it to its present shape. Before Spicer's election to Secretary he had served as a missionary on three continents; he was also Secretary of the Foreign Mission Board, and from this position he had exercised immense influence over church missions. Spicer brought this mission-mindedness into his role of Secretary. During his 19-year tenure he established the administrative infrastructure for recruiting, sending and maintaining missionaries all around the world, and made it work efficiently and effectively.

The office of Secretary expanded at the 1918 General Conference Session with the creation of the Associate Secretary position. At the same Session the duties of the Secretariat were also increased: It was now in charge of keeping minutes of church committees and collecting church statistics, as well as other duties pertinent to these responsibilities.

For his full bio see #11 of the presidents.

14. Arthur Grosvenor Daniells
May 11, 1922-May 27, 1926
(Four years)

Age when elected secretary: 63 years old
Local Conferences and Missions: 296
Ordained Ministers: 1384
Churches: 4927

Born: September 28, 1858, in West Union, Iowa
Died: March 22, 1935, in Glendale, California. He was 76 years old.

See his bio under presidents #10.

15. Cecil Kenneth Myers
May 27, 1926-October 17, 1933
(Seven years)

Age when elected secretary: 38 years old
Local Conferences and Missions: 341
Ordained Ministers: 1717
Churches: 5862

Born: August 18, 1887, in Bengal, India
Died: February 24, 1964, in Dayton, Ohio. He was 76 years old.

"I have always said that the only school from which I ever graduated was the Royal College of Colporteurs. And indeed, the colporteur work was a very integral part of my education, for when I attended college in London, England, the regular program for every student was study until twelve o'clock, noon; the dinner was served, and at one o'clock all of us went out-every young man and woman connected with the institution – with a bundle of papers or books, and sold them. We gave the whole day to this work on Sunday. Colporteuring was by far the most important subject in the curriculum, and more time was devoted to the consideration of how to reach people with our literature than to any other study." This statement was penned by Cecil Meyers in *The Youth's Instructor* of December 30, 1924.

Cecil K. Myers was sold on the colporteur work because his family became Adventists through the literature ministry. Cecil was born in Bengal, India, on August 18, 1887. His father, Herbert Benjamin Myers, was an Englishman who worked for the government of India. While living in the city of Calcutta, a colporteur, Brother Ellery Robinson, visited his home in 1898. He bought the book *Great Controversy* and later *Patriarchs and Prophets*. Cecil's mother, Mary Ellen Myers, was born in Calcutta and was a ritualist while her husband was a Baptist. The children attended two Sunday schools in order to satisfy the divided household.

However, they read the books and after follow-up Bible studies in their home, Sister Myers became the first member of the Adventist Church in India. They had four sons (Herbert, Cecil, Dudley, and Harold) who would become Adventist workers.

Cecil spent six months with his mother selling books and distributing literature in Upper Burma in 1902 and was soon followed by his father and his oldest son who opened up the Adventist work in Burma. They canvassed the Europeans and English-speaking Indians. The main religion in Burma is Buddhism. Shortly after his Burma experience Cecil left for London to attend school at Duncombe Hall Missionary College which later became Newbold College and where he wrote the paragraph in the beginning of this portrait.

On October 14, 1907, he married Ethel Hoopes, the oldest daughter of Pastor Lewis Hoopes who had been a secretary of the General Conference. From 1909 to 1917 C.K. Myers served as a minister in New South Wales and New Zealand, then in the Australasian Union Conference as secretary and vice president. In 1920 he was called to the United States as assistant secretary of the General Conference, then associate secretary, and in 1926 as secretary.

Elder C. K. Meyers would pass away in Dayton, Ohio, in 1964 at the home of his son, Dr. Kenneth Meyers, who was then a physician at Kettering Hospital.

16. Milton Earl Kern
October 17, 1933-May 26-1936
(Three years)

Age when elected Secretary: 58 years old
Local Conferences and Missions: 455
Ordained Ministers: 2247
Churches: 7640

Born: May 4, 1875, in Bedford, Indiana
Died: December 22, 1961, at Lynnwood, California. He was 86 years old.

Milton Kern became an Adventist in 1889, and in 1891 went to Union College. In 1900 he married Florence Pierce and that same year became head of the Bible and history departments of Union College. In 1893 in response to appeals from Ellen White to provide missionary opportunities for the youth of the church, he organized a "Young People's Society of Christian Service." His work in promoting missionary activities among students led the Central Union Conference to elect him secretary of the young people's department in 1904.

Kern became the first young people's secretary in the denomination. One of his first tasks was to establish young people's departments in local conferences and to train leaders. In 1907 at a special world meeting in Gland, Switzerland, a young people's department was organized and Elder Kern was named its secretary. In July of that same year, when Elder Kern met with 200 delegates on what is now the campus of Mount Vernon Academy in Ohio the name Young People's Missionary Volunteer Department was chosen for the new organization, and Elder Kern became the first Missionary Volunteer Secretary for the world church.

From 1908 to 1912 he carried the presidency of the Foreign Mission Seminary (now Washington Adventist University) along with his Missionary Volunteer duties. During the 1920s he spent most of his time overseas building the Missionary Volunteer Societies. In 1930 he was elected associate secretary of the General Conference, then became secretary in 1933.

At the 1936 GC Session, Secretary Milton Kern first used the term "Secretariat" at a Session. Kern stated in his report that year that "the Secretariat of the General Conference is charged with the responsibility of selecting and recommending to the Committee for appointment, workers for the mission fields. . ." He continued by providing a history and overview of Adventist missions. By this juncture the Secretary's Report was almost entirely concerned with missions, and the statistics and minutes his office kept enabled it to lead authoritatively in this regard.

In 1936 Elder Kern became president of the graduate school that was the forerunner of Andrews University Seminary. In 1943 he relinquished the duties of the Seminary and became field secretary of the General Conference, serving as chairman of three committees and as president of the Board of Trustees of the Ellen G. White publications. He retired in 1950 and moved to Lynnwood, California, to be near his daughter, Geneva Alcorn. In 1959 Andrews University bestowed an honorary doctorate on him (D. D.).

17. Ernest Delbert Dick
May 26, 1936-September 19, 1952
(Sixteen years)

Age when elected Secretary: 47 years old
Local Conferences and Missions: 471
Ordained Ministers: 2420
Churches: 8248

Born: December 10, 1888, in Ozawkie, Kansas
Died: July 25, 1977, in Takoma Park, Maryland. He was 88 years old.

Ernest was the son of Granville and Hannah Smalley Dick. Ernest Dick began his career of denominational service as farm manager of Union College. In 1914 he married Gertrude E. Dahl who had attended Union College. Then Elder Dick served as dean of men there. From 1915 to 1922 they were in charge of Alberta Academy in Canada which later became Canadian Union College.

They were called to Africa in 1922 where Elder Dick was principal of the Spion Kop College and later educational secretary of the South African Division. In 1932 they moved to Europe where he served as secretary of the Northern European Division. He was elected secretary of the General Conference and served in that position for sixteen years. He was president of the Seventh-day Adventist Theological Seminary for seven years until his retirement in 1959. In 1960 Andrews University granted him an honorary doctorate (D. D.). They had two children, Delbert, an anesthesiologist, and R. Eldon, an attorney.

18. Denton Edward Rebok
September 19, 1952-May 24, 1954
(Two years)

Age when elected Secretary: 55 years old
Local Conferences and Missions: 364
Ordained Ministers: 4613
Churches: 10,830

Born: April 7, 1897, in Newburg, Pennsylvania
Died: December 11, 1983, in Henderson, North Carolina. He was 86 years old.

Denton was the son of William and Anna Zimm Rebok. Both Denton Rebok and Florence Kneeland attended Washington Missionary College (Washington Adventist University today) and worked on the *Sligonian*, the college paper, together. When they graduated in 1917 they were married and almost immediately, in August 2, 1917, they sailed for the mission field of China. God blessed them with a son, Edward, and a daughter, Jean. Some eight years earlier Denton had received a tempting offer to accept money to pay for a course in dentistry in order to continue the practice of a successful doctor for whom he had worked a number of years. He chose to go to China instead.

Much of the first months in China were spent learning the language. In 1920 he began to set up an Adventist junior college and became its president. It was the first coeducational and industrial institution in China. It was a difficult job to establish a school according to Adventist concepts. Traditional Chinese education emphasized the memorization of certain revered classical texts; scholars were not to engage in manual labor, and they grew long fingernails to demonstrate this.

Professor Rebok lured his Chinese faculty and students into playing games. He began the construction of iron bed frames for the school industry. He secured agricultural machinery at a low cost from American manufacturers. He begged an automobile chassis from a New York auto show in order to begin a class in auto mechanics. In a successful effort to avoid government prohibitions on the teaching of religion in colleges, Rebok named his school the China Training Institute. He registered it with the friendly Department of Industry and Agriculture instead of the troublesome Education Department.

When World War II forced his return to the United States, he joined the faculty of Washington Missionary College and later served as president of Southern Missionary College. From 1943 to 1951 he was president of the Seventh-day Adventist Theological Seminary. He served briefly as chair of the Ellen G. White Estate Board of Trustees in 1952, and gave two presentations about Ellen G. White at the 1952 Bible Conference. These later appeared in a book called *Our Firm Foundation*.

Twelve studies on the subject of Ellen White that he presented in India to the leaders there were expanded and became the book *Believe His Prophets* which was published in 1956. He expressed his deep confidence in Ellen White as God's inspired messenger to the Adventist Church. In all he authored five books, two of which were in Chinese. He became a General Conference secretary and general field secretary. In 1962 Andrews University granted him an honorary doctorate (D. D.).

On June 28, 1976, his wife Florence passed away and Elder Rebok later married Marie Opsahl Burrows. Rebok's last four years before retirement were spent at La Sierra College as a professor of sociology and religion. Denton and Marie set up the Rebok Estate which after his death provided a gift to the Seventh-day Adventist Church for Adventist World Radio-Asia and established a library at the church's world headquarters. The library, in the atrium of the headquarters, is called the Rebok Memorial Library.

19. Walter Raymond Beach
May 24, 1954–June 11, 1970
(Sixteen years)

Age when elected Secretary: 52 years old
Local Conferences and Missions: 348
Ordained Ministers: 5039
Churches: 11,447

Born: January 18, 1902, in St. John, North Dakota
Died: December 10, 1994, in Loma Linda, California. He was 92 years old.

Walter Raymond Beach was born in the middle of a snowstorm in January on his family's windswept farm in North Dakota, a few miles south of the Canadian border. He was the last child born of Herbert and Margaret Milliken Beach. Walter graduated from Gem State Academy and then Walla Walla College in 1923. While at Walla Walla he met Gladys I. Corley, a Texas girl of Baptist parents.

Gladys had been sent to Laurelwood Academy and Walla Walla College by her Adventist aunt, Attie Chandler. She would become an elementary school teacher. Walter and Gladys were married on August 9, 1923, in Albany, Oregon. Elder Beach began denominational work as a Bible teacher and principal at Auburn Adventist Academy in Washington. He was ordained in New York City in 1926 on his way to Europe. After his ordination, he began a twenty-seven-year ministry in Europe.

Though Elder Beach had studied Spanish and expected to be sent to Spain, they were sent to Paris, France, where for a year he engaged in French language and culture study almost day and night at the Sorbonne (University of Paris). Knowing that the French were obsessively fussy about the pronunciation and use of their language-especially lampooning the English slaughter of the guttural French *r*-Beach hired a retired French actress to coach him in mastering the pointed French vowels and the diabolic *r*. He would trudge up and down the narrow hallways of their tiny flat gargling gulps of water in order to master the rolling sound of that telltale consonant. A year later he spoke French with barely a trace of the famous drawl with which most Americans give themselves away if they learn to speak French as adults.

Beach began as youth and education director at the old Latin Union Conference with headquarters in Gland, Switzerland. He was just twenty-six years old when he was asked to be president of the Belgian Conference and three years later president of the Franco-Belgian Union with headquarters in Paris. In between work he went to the University of Paris (Sorbonne) and took additional language studies and devoured books on French theologians. Two girls (Jo Ray and Colette) and a boy (Dr. Bert B. Beach, for many years the director of Religious Liberty at the General Conference) were born overseas. He began to speak French with power and elegance and wrote three books and many articles in French.

He was later elected secretary and then president of the Southern European Division with headquarters in Bern, Switzerland. During World War II, on top of his administrative responsibilities, Beach became editor of the French *Life and Health* magazine. And since the division office was cut off from its French-speaking base in France, he sometimes had to write several articles in the same issue. For a while he worked with the Swiss Broadcasting Corporation at night as a speaker for the news on shortwave. They beamed news to America from Switzerland. Mrs. Beach even prepared children's programs that were beamed to America.

Elder Beach's presidency continued a postwar rebuilding and expansion of the worship and educational facilities of the church in Europe. In 1954 he was elected secretary of the General Conference and returned to America. In 1954 the honorary degree of doctor of laws was conferred upon him by his alma mater, Walla Walla College. He served as secretary until 1970. During this period he was instrumental in launching the first Global Mission program, entitled "From Everywhere to Everywhere." Beach, by now recognized as an expert in church organization, served five more years as a General Conference general vice president and retired in 1975.

Beach had won several oratorical contests as a youth and an Idaho Senator had offered to sponsor him to a prestigious university. His parents refused to take advantage of this free education and paid for him to go to Walla Walla College since they had dedicated him to the ministry before he was born. Standing at only 5'2" he had learned to be an expert orator and a quick thinker on his feet. Once at a large GC meeting he raised his hand to be recognized to speak. The chairman saw his hand in the back and called on him saying, "Elder Beach, will you please stand so we can see you better?" To which Beach replied, "Mr. Chairman, I am standing!" The audience laughter prepared the way for the point he was about to make.

He was a prolific writer. His best seller, *Nous and Nos Enfants,* was first written in French and then translated into a dozen languages. His best-known books in English are *Dimensions in Salvation* and *Light from God's Lamp*. His last book was authored with his son Bert, *Pattern for Progress* and dealt with the organization of the church. Walter Raymond Beach passed away in Loma Linda, California, in 1994.

20. Clyde Ora Franz
June 11, 1970-April 16, 1980
(Ten years)

Age when elected Secretary: 57 years
Local Conferences and Missions: 378
Ordained Ministers: 7381
Churches: 16,505

Born: March 1, 1913, in Camaguey, Cuba.
Retired: Living in North Carolina. He is 102 (2015) years old and still counting.

Five children were born to Lucile and Charles Franz. Clyde, the only boy, was the firstborn. Mildred, Maisie, Lovey (died as an infant), and Theresa would follow. In 1910 Lucile and Charles were married and left almost immediately for Cuba as self-supporting missionaries. Then they joined a group that established a boarding school for black youth at Hillcrest, Tennessee. Charles Franz would serve as treasurer, secretary and book manager for the next 36 years, working in four different conferences and the Southern Union. He was also the financial adviser for Oakwood College and Riverside Sanitarium.

Clyde Franz earned an accounting degree at Southern Missionary College in 1932. Like his father, Clyde went on to serve as secretary-treasurer of several Adventist conferences, including Alabama-Mississippi, Kentucky-Tennessee, Iowa, and the British West Indies Union. He was ordained to the ministry in Kingston, Jamaica, in 1946. In the 1950s he returned to his birthplace and served in the Antillean Union, based in Cuba, for two years as president.

From 1954 to 1961 Clyde was the secretary of the Inter-American Division, based in Miami, Florida. He also served there as treasurer until 1966. At the 1966 General Conference session in Detroit, Michigan, Robert Pierson, his college classmate, was elected president of the Adventist Church. "Hey, Bob," he remembers joking at a chance meeting in Cobo Hall, "if you ever need a janitor there someday, remember me." Pierson knew Franz's abilities to work with people and to keep records and called him, not as a janitor, but to be an associate executive secretary. Four years later he was appointed secretary.

God has blessed Elder Franz with long life. At his last birthday he turned 102 and is still sharp of intellect. He has outlived three wives. Four months after they celebrated their 50th wedding anniversary, Lois Mae Clark Franz passed away. Lois Mae served as a teacher, organist and secretary all over the world with her husband. They had two children, Charles and Sue. His second wife, a nurse, Eulalia White, passed away in 1997, and his third wife Joyce Rochat, a professor of English at Andrews University, passed away in 2003. Franz says that although he enjoyed each marriage, he will remain a bachelor. He walks two to three miles every day, is a vegetarian and feels that the Sabbath has been a great blessing to him. In 1974 Andrews University granted him an honorary doctorate (D. D.).

In 1973, a new General Conference Archives was founded, and in 1975 it was combined with the Statistical Secretary's bureau to form the Office of Archives and Statistics, answering to the Secretary. In 2011, it was renamed Office of Archives, Statistics, and Research, answering to the Executive Secretary, who thus has ultimate responsibility for institutional research, as well as keeping documentary and statistical records.

At the General Conference Session of 1975 the position of Undersecretary was instituted. The Undersecretary assists the Secretary with his responsibilities and acts for him in his absence; serves as the agenda secretary for the General Conference Session, Annual Council, Spring Meeting, and officers' meetings; is responsible for the General Conference *Working Policy*; provides oversight to administrative and personnel matters within the office of the Secretariat; and serves as secretary or member of various standing committees as well as the liaison for one of the world divisions.

100th birthday

21. George Ralph Thompson
April 16, 1980-June 29, 2000
(Twenty years)

Age when elected Secretary: 51 years old
Local Conferences and Missions: 376
Ordained Ministers: 9,423
Churches: 21,555

Born: March 20, 1929, in Connell Town, St. Lucy Parish, Barbados
Retired: Living in Florida. In 2015 he was 86 years old.

Because his father's name was George Ralph Thompson also, they called his little son G. Ralph to avoid confusion. His mother, Edna, and brother and two half-sisters were active members of the Pilgrim Holiness Church and his parents were lay preachers there. He began his early education at the Selah Boys School, a government elementary school. Life was pretty good for young G. Ralph in Barbados until he got to secondary school.

G. Ralph was academically at the top of his class and had demonstrated that he was an excellent and gifted student eager to excel in all of his studies. When his family moved he transferred from Leeward High School, a private school, to the government operated Parry School. After just a short while as a student in the new school he was informed that his age was a problem. He was sixteen and the school did not accept new students over the age of sixteen. He was informed that he would be dismissed.

In the meantime, G. Ralph's brother who was a tailor met an Adventist tailor, Fred Graves, who gave him a copy of *The Marked Bible*. He passed this book to G. Ralph and it caught his attention so much that he asked for other books and was given *The Great Controversy* and the rest of the books in the *Conflict of the Ages* series.

Then he was told that the principal of the Caribbean Training College in Trinidad (at that time it was a high school and junior college offering the first two years of college. Today it is the University of the

Southern Caribbean) would be in Barbados recruiting students. He arranged for an interview with the Adventist principal, took an exam and was admitted into the school despite his mother's protest. An Adventist school in Trinidad was the last thing his evangelist mother wanted for her son. G. Ralph prayed for Divine Wisdom to enable him to convince his mother about the school, and with his prayer answered, off he went to Trinidad.

In March, 1946, he began school at Caribbean Training College. The Holy Spirit touched his heart as he continued to read the books and in September he was baptized into the Adventist Church at age 17. He worked very hard to pay his tuition and also had some fun singing in a popular men's group called the College Heralds. The College Heralds was composed of talented male junior college students who hoped to musically enrich church services as well as bless the evangelistic programs conducted around Trinidad. The College Heralds toured Barbados and gave concerts to raise money for Christian education. G. Ralph finished his last year of high school and first two years of college at Caribbean Training College graduating on December 3, 1950.

From 1950 to 1953 he worked as a pastoral intern in Trinidad and Tobago. He came to America in 1954 and attended Atlantic Union College to complete his last two years. He graduated from Atlantic Union College in 1956 with a Bachelor of Art in Religion with a minor in history. He studied at the Adventist Seminary in Washington, D. C., and got his Master's degree in 1958. Elder Jonathan Roach, the Education Director from the Lake Region Conference, called Thompson to teach there and he worked for a short time with Elder Thomas M. Rowe as an assistant pastor at the same time that he was principal of the Cassopolis, Michigan, church school.

He met Imogene Baker, a nurse also from Barbados, and they were married on July 19, 1959.He attended the Adventist Seminary in Washington and then returned to Caribbean Union College where he was the Bible teacher and pastor of the college church. Elder Thompson was ordained to the gospel ministry December 5, 1960. He returned to the States and completed graduate work at Andrews University. He began his ministry in the South Caribbean Conference. Between 1962 and 1964, he was chairperson of the Theology Department at his Alma Mater, the Caribbean Union College in Trinidad. From there he was elected president of the East Caribbean Conference headquartered in Barbados and stayed six years in that post.

Eventually Thompson was called to the Caribbean Union with headquarters in Trinidad from 1970 to 1975 as the first West Indian born president. In addition to providing strong administrative leadership, for nearly 20 years he was the main speaker of a very popular weekly religious radio program broadcast over Radio Barbados called Faith for Today. Thousands listened to the program which resulted in numerous listeners becoming Adventists after completing the correspondence course that was offered. Many attended evangelistic meetings as a result of the radio program.

In 1975, at the General Conference session in Vienna, Austria, he was elected associate secretary and vice president of the General Conference, the first non-white person to hold this position. When Elder Robert Pierson's health failed and he had to retire in 1979, Elder Thompson served as acting president of the world church for six months. In 1980 he was elected Executive Secretary of the world church, the first non-white person and the first person from the Inter-American Division to be elected to this office.

Elder Thompson was a bold and powerful evangelist and preacher. Many said that they enjoyed the reports that he gave at the General Conference and at the year-end meetings because he was the secretary who preached his reports and made them exciting. The Thompson's have three children, one son Gerald, two daughters, Carol Jean and Linda Mae. In 1983 Andrews University granted him an honorary doctorate (D. D.). In 2014 the University of the Southern Caribbean in Trinidad and Tobago conferred an Honorary Doctoral degree on him. Pastor Thompson has received many other awards over the years and presently lives in Florida and serves as one of the pastors of the church he attends.

22. Matthew Ango Bediako
June 29, 2000-June 23, 2010
(Ten years)

Age when elected Secretary: 57 years old
Local Conferences and Missions: 489
Ordained Ministers: 13,971
Churches: 48,933

Born: October 24, 1942, in Bekwai, Ghana
Retired: Living in Ghana. He is 72 years old (2015).

Matthew Bediako's ancestors practiced paganism and idol worship. His grandfather was a fetish priest in the rural village of Kotwia in the Bekwai area of the Asante Region of Ghana. His parents, Mr. and Mrs. Kwasi Ango, saw to it that their children attended Adventists schools in the area and a new life with Christ emerged for Matthew.

Matthew was greatly influenced by African American missionaries Johnny and Ida Johnson who made the work of God very attractive and meaningful for young people at the Bekwai Secondary School and Teacher Training College. Matthew would translate for the missionaries when they preached in the villages.

Young Matthew chose to study for the ministry at the Adventist College of West Africa (now Babcock University) in Nigeria. When he graduated in 1967 he was hired as an Adventist worker and stationed at his old compound of Bekwai as a Bible teacher and pastor of the college church. While there he married Elizabeth Lydia Coffie, a soloist and seamstress, on February 4, 1968. God blessed them with four daughters.

In 1973 Bediako was ordained to the gospel ministry. His administrative abilities were recognized and he soon became president of the Central Ghana Conference. He was then appointed to the position of president for the West African Union, replacing S. B. Johansen. This was the first time that an African had been appointed to the position of president for the West African Union. At the GC session in New Orleans he became a general field secretary (1986) and then a general vice-president for the World Church (1990-2000).

At the 57th General Conference in Toronto, Canada, in 2000, Pastor Bediako was elected to the second highest position in the Adventist Church. Being the first African to hold this office, Bediako has received many awards. In 2001 Andrews University granted him an honorary doctorate (D. D.).He has received three honorary degrees and the leaders of Kenya, the Gambia, and Malawi have given him awards for service. Perhaps the most meaningful award that he received was from his own country. In 2006 Pastor Bediako was awarded the "Order of the Volta" from Ghana's president, John Agyekum Kufuor. During the country's first-ever National Honours Day two members of the Bediako family were recognized. Pastor Bediako's older brother, Thomas Ango Bediako, a longtime educator and leader of teachers, also received the "Order of the Volta."

During the 1990s, responsibility for mission diversified in the Secretariat, with the establishment of new entities, including the Offices of Global Mission and of Mission Awareness—the two were merged in 2005 as Adventist Mission. But by 2010 it had become plain that more collaboration and unity of purpose was needed in the church's mission enterprise.

After the 2010 General Conference Session, all the General Conference's mission-related entities were placed under the direct jurisdiction of the Executive Secretary: Adventist Mission, Institute of World Mission, Adventist Volunteer Service, and International Personnel Resources and Services (for which the Secretary shares responsibility with the Treasurer). In 2012, the Office of Membership Software was created, and placed within the Secretariat.

23. Gan Theow Ng
June 23, 2010-

Age when elected Secretary: 61 years old
Local Conferences and Missions: 585
Ordained Ministers: 17,272
Churches: 70,188

Born: October 20, 1948, in Singapore
Current Executive Secretary. 66 years old (2015) and still counting.

"GT", as he is affectionately called by his colleagues and friends, is currently serving the Seventh-day Adventist world church as its executive secretary, a position he has held since the 2010 General Conference Session. Previously, Ng worked as an associate secretary for the world church, where he oversaw the Church's Northern Asia-Pacific, Southern Asia, and Trans-European divisions.

GT's denominational service began in the 1970s in Cambodia, where ministry in the war-torn country first kindled his enthusiasm for mission. Shortly before Phnom Penh fell to Khmer Rouge forces, Ng and his wife were evacuated from Cambodia. Later, Ng served in Thailand, Malaysia, and his native Singapore, where he was a pastor, health educator, and union departmental director.

From 1991 to 2000 Ng served as professor and dean of the Theological Seminary at the Adventist International Institute of Advanced Studies (AIIAS) in the Philippines. In 2000, Ng accepted a call to be the executive secretary of the church's Southern Asia-Pacific Division.

Ng moved to the Washington, D.C. area in 2004 to serve as a world church associate secretary at the General Conference. Ng spurred numerous church membership audits, challenging church officials world-wide to reconcile membership tallies with actual church attendance. He also encouraged missionaries to serve in regions of acute need, including the 10/40 Window – a region spanning from West Africa across Asia and covering two-thirds of the world's population where only 1 percent is Christian.

Ng holds a bachelor's degree from Southeast Asia Union College in Singapore. His post-graduate work includes a master's degree from the Adventist Theological Seminary in the Philippines and a Ph.D. degree from the Theological Seminary at Andrews University in Berrien Springs, Michigan.

Dr. Ng was elected chair of the Ellen G. White Estate Board of Trustees in 2014. He is the twelfth person to hold the position since Ellen White named five trustees to oversee her literary estate at the time of her death in 1915. He follows Don Schneider and is the first person from Asia to chair the board.

Ng and his wife, Ivy (Mee Jee Foo) Ng, who works for the Hope Channel, have two married children, Jocelyn and Mervyn.

Today, the Secretariat's responsibilities can be summarized thus:

· Coordination of mission-related activities to create synergy and move forward the mission enterprise of the Seventh-day Adventist Church.

· The selection and appointment of international and volunteer personnel for all calls between divisions, as well as providing support, promotion and strategic input for the mission program of the church.

· The preparation of agendas as well as the writing and preservation of minutes of major General Conference administrative committees. Associated with this responsibility is coordinating the development and review of *General Conference Working Policy* as well as the *Church Manual*.

· The operation of the General Conference archives, and the production of the world church's *Annual Statistical Report* and *Yearbook*. Administrative liaison for the General Conference to all world divisions.

Interesting Facts about the GC Secretaries and Treasurers

The first Secretary was Uriah Smith, elected on the same day as the General Conference was incorporated. Smith went on to be the longest-serving Secretary overall (22 years in all, in four separate periods), with G. Ralph Thompson serving twenty years, the most consecutive years (1980-2000). Executive Secretaries (as the second highest position in the Church is now called) continue to be elected at General Conference Sessions, which since 1970, have been held every five years.

In 1871 Adelia Patten Van Horn became treasurer of the General Conference-the first woman to serve as a General Conference officer. Her husband, Isaac, was also treasurer six years before her, making them the only husband and wife to serve as treasurer.

-In 1875 Frederika House (Sisley) was elected treasurer of the General Conference. She was the second woman and, at age 22, the youngest and only single person ever elected as an officer of the church.

-In 1877 Minerva J. Chapman became the third and last woman to be elected to the post of General Conference Treasurer. Her brother, John N. Loughborough, also served as treasurer, making them the only brother and sister to serve as treasurer.

-No woman has ever been elected to the Office of Secretary of the church.

-Uriah Smith is the only person to serve as both treasurer and secretary of the church.

-Uriah Smith served four separate times as treasurer for a total of nearly 22 years.

-G. Ralph Thompson served as secretary longer than anyone else in continuous service- 20 consecutive years.

-G. Ralph Thompson, born in Barbados, was the first black person to serve as an officer of the church.

-Matthew Bediako, born in Ghana, was the first African to serve as secretary.

G. T. Ng, born in Singapore, is the first Asian to serve as secretary.

-On March 1, 2015, Clyde Franz turned 102 years old, making him the secretary who lived the longest. Three secretaries died quite young: Howard E. Osborne at 34; Charles W. Stone at 35 in a train crash; and Dan T. Jones at age 46.

-Six of the secretaries were not born in the United States. A.B. Oyen was born in Norway, C.K. Meyers in India, C.O. Franz in Cuba, G. R. Thompson in Barbados, M. A. Bediako in Ghana, and G. T. Ng in Singapore.

All of the Treasurers were born in the United States except Lance Butler who was born in Australia, Robert Lemon, the son of a Canadian missionary, who was born in Zaire, and Juan Prestol-Puesan who was born in the Dominican Republic.

Treasurer Kenneth Emerson's daughter, Anita, married Robert Folkenberg who would become president. Therefore, Anita's father was a General Conference treasurer and her husband was a General Conference president.

At 68, Juan Prestol-Puesan was the oldest person to be elected Treasurer.

At 63, A. G. Daniells, was the oldest person to be elected Secretary.

Treasury Dept at the GC 2014

TREASURERS

—๛—

1. E. S. Walker 1863-1865
2. I. D. Van Horn.....................1865-1868
3. J N. Loughborough 1868-1869
4. E.S. Walker 1869-1870
5. G.H. Bell 1870 1871
6. Mrs. A. P. Van Horn 1871-1873
7. E.B. Gaskill........................1873-1874
8. Harmon Lindsay..................1874 1875
9. Frederika House 1875-1878
10. Uriah Smith.......................1878-1877
11. Mrs. M. J. Chapman..........1877-1883
12. A.R. Henry 1883-1888
13. Harmon Lindsay...............1888-1893
14. W.H. Edwards 1893-1897

15. A. G. Adams......................1897-1900
16. H. M. Mitchell...................1901-1903
17. I. H. Evans........................1903-1909
18. W.T. Knox 1909-1922
19. I. L. Shaw.........................1922-1936
20. W. E. Nelson 1936-1950
21. C.L. Torrey........................1950-1968
22. K. H. Emmerson 1968-1980
23. L.L. Butler........................1980-1985
24. Donald F. Gilbert...............1985-1995
25. Robert L. Rawson 1995-2002
26. Robert E. Lemon...............2002-2015
27. Juan Prestol-Puesan 2015-

THE TREASURY DEPARTMENT

Early denominational treasurers did not take on the treasury responsibility on a full-time basis. To be Treasurer of the General Conference was a minor responsibility that was tacked onto whatever else that person was doing. Most times the person who was the business manager or a respected worker of the Review and Herald Publishing Association added this small task to his/her portfolio. Early treasurers tended to be young and served short periods of time (one to three years). Later treasurers tended to accept the position after acquiring real financial skills and so were older and served for longer periods of time.

The growing size of the church and its increasing revenues called for more skilled money management. As the tithing system was adopted and implemented, effective policies that assured workers their salaries even during severe financial reversals and protected church money from rapidly fluctuating inflation had to be enacted. Appeals from the pulpit each Sabbath morning for the needs of the local church and its foreign mission program ceased to be sufficient.

Today the world church budget is in the billions of dollars and must respect the complicated laws imposed on it by the many governmental regulations and laws. Besides the Treasurer, the treasury staff now includes a fulltime Undertreasurer and many fulltime associate and assistant treasurers who are each experts in certain areas of finance.

1. Eli S. Walker
May 21, 1863-May 17, 1865
(Two years)

Age when elected Treasurer: 37 years old
Total Tithes when elected: $8,000
Per capita giving when elected: $2.29

Born: December 16, 1825, probably in Pennsylvania
Died: September 16, 1907, near Mountain View, California. He was 81 years old.

Eli S. Walker was the first General Conference treasurer and also the fourth. He was born December 16, 1825. He and his wife Eliza Norton Walker lived in Pennsylvania before migrating to Iowa. As a young man, Eli had been a member of the Brethren Church and then a member of the Methodist Church.

The Walkers united with the Seventh-day Adventist Church at Knoxville, Iowa, in 1858. After joining the Church Eli became a pioneer Adventist worker and organizer in Iowa. In 1860 Elder James White called him from Iowa to Battle Creek, Michigan, and Brother Walker became the secretary and treasurer of the Review and Herald Publishing Company. He served for nine years in these positions.

Walker was well known by the Battle Creek members when he was elected at age thirty-seven to become the first treasurer of the newly-organized Adventist Church whose membership at that time was estimated to be 3500. Since he was already the treasurer at the Review and Herald it was natural for him to take on this additional responsibility. Probably his main work at the Review and Herald was more time-consuming and more challenging than setting up and keeping the books of the emerging Adventist Church. As far as we know, Walker was a layman and was never ordained as a minister.

He had three children. His two daughters, Nora and Marietta Walker, became the first typesetting girls employed by the Review. Nora would marry Egbert C. Loughborough, a nephew of John Loughborough, and Marietta would marry Homer Aldrich, son of Jotham Aldrich, who was the president of the Review and Herald and had served as chairman of the first General Conference session.

Eli Walker became deaf in later life and died on September 16, 1907, at age eighty-one near Mountain View, California, in his son-in-law and daughter's home (E. C. and Nora Loughborough).

Treasury note 1866

2. Isaac Doren Van Horn
May 17, 1865-May 12, 1868
(Three years)

Age when elected Treasurer: 31 years old
Total Tithes when elected: $12,000
Per capita giving when elected: $3.00

Born: March 28, 1834, in Cato, New York.
Died: August 22, 1910. He was 76 years old.

Isaac's family moved to Michigan in September, 1844 where he first heard of the soon coming of Christ. He spent his youth there and attended Albion College. While teaching school in 1859, he attended a series of meetings held in a schoolhouse by Elder Joseph Bates. After hearing two discourses, he decided to keep the Sabbath. He began preaching in 1863 and was ordained to the gospel ministry the following year. Elder J. N. Andrews gave the charge, and Elder James White offered the prayer.

At age 31 two important events happened to him. In April, 1865, he was united in marriage to Ms. Adelia Patten. They were married by James White at the Battle Creek church. In May, 1865, he was elected treasurer of the General Conference and served from 1865 to 1868. The Van Horns were the only workers in which both the husband and wife served as treasurers of the General Conference. They had three sons: Burt, Newman, and Charles Wesley Van Horn.

Elder Van Horn proved to be a good evangelist and in 1863 was requested to go to the Pacific Coast to labor. In 1874, responding to requests for ministerial help from Adventist members in the Walla Walla Valley, he went to the state of Washington and established a church in Walla Walla. His efforts in Walla Walla led to the conversion of Alonzo T. Jones. He was also the first Adventist minister to work in Oregon. He remained on the West Coast for eight years working in California,

Oregon, and Washington. Two conferences of 300 members each were organized and he became the president of the newly formed North Pacific Conference.

On his return to Michigan, Elder I. D. Van Horn preached at camp meetings and among the churches. He served as president of the Michigan Conference from 1888 to 1891. Then until 1898 he traveled extensively in Eastern Canada and the Eastern States. Returning to Battle Creek in 1898, he was engaged mostly in church work in that city and in Michigan. In 1907, while working in his garden, he suffered from sunstroke and was incapacitated until the time of his death on August 22, 1910. He was 76 years old.

3. John Norton Loughborough
May 12 1868-May 18, 1869
(One year)

Age when elected Treasurer: 36 years old
Total Tithes when elected: $23,366.57
Per capita giving when elected: $5.22

Born: January 26, 1832, in Victor, New York.
Died: April 7, 1924, at St. Helena, California. He was 92 years old.

John became a Christian at an early age, and began preaching for the First-day Adventists when only sixteen years old. He painted houses during the week. In 1852 a member of one of his congregations, who had become interested in the truths being taught by Sabbatarian Adventists, invited Loughborough to attend one of the Sabbatarian conferences with him.

Although only twenty years of age, Loughborough had already been preaching for over three years and was confident that he could defeat the Sabbatarians with a few texts showing the moral law had been abolished. However, the speaker for the evening was J. N. Andrews. Andrews used the same texts Loughborough had prepared to use against the law, but used them to show the Christian's continuing obligation to keep the law. Within three weeks Loughborough had decided to cast his lot with the Sabbatarian Adventists. He began at once to preach this message to others.

He was ordained to the gospel ministry at Grand Rapids, Michigan, in 1853. At age 36, in May, 1868, he was elected to be the treasurer of the General Conference. At the same meetings, with Elder D. T. Bourdeau, he was selected by the General Conference to pioneer evangelistic work on the Pacific Coast. They left Battle Creek, Michigan, later that year, going by way of the Isthmus of Panama, and reaching San Francisco on July 18, 1868. By 1871 they helped establish five churches in Sonoma County, one of them in Santa Rosa, where the first Adventist Church building west of the Rockies was erected in 1869. He baptized the first three Adventist members in Nevada in 1878.

That same year Elder Loughborough was requested to take charge of the denominational work in Great Britain, where he and his second wife, Maggie, remained five years. Afterward he traveled in many of the European fields.

In 1908, at the age of 76, he began a tour of the world, visiting the principal centers of the Seventh-day Adventist work in Hawaii, New Zealand, Australia, Africa, and Europe. On this extended journey he traveled about 36,000 miles by water, and 6000 miles by land. After he returned to the States in 1883 he settled in Lodi, California, where his daughter, Mrs. J. J. (Mary) Ireland, was then living. As a representative of the General Conference he made short trips to camp meetings, institutions, and general meetings strengthening members who had become confused because of apostate movements.

He served as president of the Michigan Conference from 1865 to 1868, and then the treasurer of the General Conference from 1868 to 1869. He was the first president of the California Conference (1890-1896; again, 1887-1890), and of the Nevada Association (1878), the Upper Columbia Conference (1884-1885), and of the Illinois Conference (1891-1895).

He was the author of many books and publications. In 1892 he published *The Rise and Progress of Seventh-day Adventists*, the first denominational history and in 1907 *The Church, Its Organization, Order, and Discipline*, which for many years served as the church manual. Elder Loughborough passed away peacefully at the St. Helena Sanitarium, on April 7, 1924, at age 92.

4. Eli Walker
May 18, 1869-March 15, 1870
(One year)

Age when elected Treasurer (Second Time): 43 years old
Total Tithes when elected: $18,952.77
Per capita giving when elected: $3.87

For bio and picture see number 1.

5. Goodloe Harper Bell
March 15, 1870-February 7, 1871
(One year)

Age when elected Treasurer: 37 years old
Total Tithes when elected: $21,822.46
Per capita giving when elected: $4.01

Born: April 7, 1832, in Watertown, New York.
Died: January 17, 1899. He was 66 years of age.

Goodloe Bell was the eldest of 12 children born to David and Lucy Blodgett Bell. He allegedly studied at Oberlin College. Later he moved west with his family to Michigan.

At age 19 he taught his first country school. He worked as an inspector of schools in the counties around Grand Rapids from 1854 to the mid-1860s. Declining health, the death of his wife and overwork placed him in the Battle Creek Sanitarium, where he heard and accepted the Adventist faith. He had been a Baptist and for a time a Disciple of Christ.

When his health improved he began a private school for Adventist children in the Battle Creek community. His students included William and Edson White, sons of James and Ellen White, and the Kellogg brothers, Will K. and John Harvey. The study in which he most delighted was that of nature; and often he would go many miles to find one specimen of a plant or flower that he set his heart on critically examining. He was also interested in painting, architecture, and music.

While teaching school, Bell also edited the *Youth's Instructor*. Beginning in 1869 he became superintendent of the Battle Creek Sabbath School, and served as General Conference Treasurer between March 1870 and February 1871. He also was one of the directors of the Health Institute. On December 10, 1871, Ellen White was given a vision in which she saw "Bell in connection with the cause and work of God in Battle Creek."

Bell was a strict disciplinarian, which brought both approval and criticism from parents and students. By 1872 Bell had left Battle Creek, discouraged about his reputation. He became principal of the newly established South Lancaster Academy in Massachusetts which later became Atlantic Union College. But Ellen White wrote, urging him to return to teach in the school that was to open that year.

On June 3, 1872, twelve students went up to the second story of the old Review print shop, where Bell welcomed them. The school was a success from the beginning, and in December 1874, it was moved to the newly erected Battle Creek College. Bell headed the English Department, under Sydney Brownsberger, president. Bell is known as a prominent author of school textbooks. In his later years, Bell started the first church correspondence school and had a profound and lasting influence on the development of the church's Sabbath School program.

While Bell was riding from his country home into the city of Battle Creek, on January 10, 1899, his horse ran away, and he met with an accident which resulted in his early death. He died on January 17, 1899. He was 66 years of age. For many years his influence continued through the numerous books that he had published.

6. Adelia Parlance Patten Van Horn
February 7, 1871-March 11, 1873
(Two years)

Age when elected Treasurer: 31 years old
Total Tithes when elected: $23,066.42
Per capita giving when elected: $5.07

Born: June 30, 1839, in Onondago County, New York
Died: July 8, 1922, at Battle Creek, Michigan. She was 83 years old.

Adelia was the daughter of Levi Curtis and Adelia Patten. She grew up in a family of six children and heard her mother pray for each child by name daily. She was baptized at Battle Creek, Michigan, by Elder James White in 1861 and immediately she entered his home assisting Sister White in the preparation of many of her writings for publication. Her mother and father soon joined the Adventist Church in 1862 and were faithful Adventists until their deaths. Later in life she was connected with the Battle Creek College and the Sanitarium, and still later served as editor of the *Youth's Instructor*. Her marriage to Elder Isaac D. Van Horn occurred on April 29, 1865. They had three sons: Burt, Newman, and Charles Wesley (who died at age 28).

Not having any daughters of her own, Sister White felt very close to Adelia and called Adelia her daughter. When the Van Horns moved west to pioneer the work there, Mrs. White braved the rough seas to visit Adelia and her family. Adelia once wrote, "We still hold your visit in grateful remembrance, and hope you will come again. . . [Our little son] Burtie often asks, 'What makes her stay away so long?' He still calls the room you occupied, Grandma White's room, for it brings back such pleasant recollections every time he speaks thus."

Elder I. D. Van Horn and his wife, Adelia Van Horn, both held, at different times, the position of Treasurer of the General Conference. Adelia served as treasurer for two years, from February 7, 1871 to March 11, 1873. She would be the first woman to serve as a General Conference officer. During their forty-five years of married life Adelia traveled with her husband from field to field, ably assisting him in his work of spreading the gospel. She was left a widow in 1910. Her death occurred at Battle Creek, Michigan, July 8, 1922.

7. Elijah B. Gaskell
March 11, 1873-August 10, 1874
(One year)

Age when elected Treasurer: 39 years old
Total Tithes when elected: $30,687.49
Per capita giving when elected: $5.22

Born: May 4, 1833, in Niagara Falls, New York
Died: March 8, 1909, at Hildebrand, North Carolina. He was 75 years of age.

Elijah Gaskell (sometimes spelled Gaskill) was born near Niagara Falls, New York, in 1833. Born of godly parents, he took an active interest in religious things. In 1861 he married Mary Lindsay whose parents were among the pioneers of the message in New York State. He was a successful worker in the New York Conference for many years until he was called by the General Conference to Battle Creek, Michigan, to be treasurer.

In 1891 he married Jenny England. In 1893 he was called to work in South Africa, where he did faithful ship missionary work for ten years, returning in 1903 to this country because of bad health. His wife Jenny was a cook at Claremont College while he canvassed and spread Adventist literature.

Brother Gaskell was very active in South Africa. At the seaports he visited thousands of steamships, mail boats, sailing vessels, and warships. He sold books, tracts, and health literature and gave away papers by the thousands. He also visited war camps in the Boer War and hospitals in Cape Town. The officers, doctors, and nurses often expressed thankfulness for the good literature that he distributed and the patients would stretch out thin, feeble hands for the papers. When their youngest child, Luther, died in Africa they adopted a little girl to be with their two daughters.

When they moved to North Carolina he acted as a solicitor for the Piedmont Sanitarium. Jenny lived for thirty-nine years after the death of her husband and died at the age of ninety years.

8. Harmon Lindsay
August 10, 1874-August 15, 1875
(One year)

Age when elected Treasurer: 38 years old
Total Tithes when elected: $31,000
Per capita giving when elected: $4.43

Born: August 14, 1835, in Newfane, New York
Died: March 7, 1918, in Olcott, New York. He was 82 years old.

Harmon Lindsay came from a very distinguished family of Adventists. His father, John M. Lindsay, and mother, Eliza A. Taylor Lindsay, were early Adventists from Olcott, New York, who entertained many of the earliest pioneers including John Andrews and John Loughborough. His nephew, Harmon William Lindsay, was an outstanding professor and educational administrator. He married Tamar Gaskell whose father had been a General Conference treasurer. Harmon grew up in the church and when the family moved to Battle Creek he became an elder of the Battle Creek church and member of the General Conference executive committee.

In 1874 he was elected to a one-year term as General Conference treasurer. Thirteen years later he was elected to another five years as General Conference treasurer. He was a part of the three-man team that went to Huntsville, Alabama, to seek out a place for the development of a school for black Adventists. Two presidents, Elders G.A. Irwin and O.A. Olson, who were a part of the three-man team, felt deeply impressed walking under the sixty-five towering oaks that stood where what was to become the heart of the campus of Oakwood University.

Harmon participated in the establishment and development of Battle Creek College and served as treasurer of several other church institutions, among them the Review and Herald Publishing Association. While in Australia, Ellen White entrusted her business affairs to Lindsay.

Harmon joined with A. R. Henry to promote shrewd business deals. They operated the Review as a business rather than as an instrument to promote the Adventist message. They were more concerned about printing Montgomery Ward's catalogs than religious books. Mrs. White reprimanded these two financial leaders and said that their dealings were becoming more and more secular. After being an Adventist for more than forty years Harmon Lindsay finally left the Adventist Church and became a Christian Scientist. He died a Christian Scientist and is buried in West Lake Road Cemetery.

9. Frederika House Sisley
August 15, 1875-September 1976
(One year)

Age when elected Treasurer: 22 years old
Total Tithes when elected: $32,618.62
Per capita giving when elected: $4.06

Born: October 7, 1852, near Elmira, New York
Died: January 25, 1934, in Nashville, Tennessee. She was 81 years old.

The 1875 nominating committee recommended the name of "Miss Freddie House" for treasurer. The capable young lady had impressed everyone at the fourteenth session of the General Conference and her name was unanimously accepted. She would be the second woman and the only single person to hold the position of treasurer and an officer of the General Conference.

When Frederika was seven years old some of her sisters joined the Seventh-day Adventist Church. She learned from them the message of Adventism. At eighteen she went to Iowa to teach public school and two years later was persuaded by her relatives to attend the newly opened college at Battle Creek, Michigan. While a student there, she gave her heart to God.

Frederika served as secretary-treasurer of the Review and Herald Publishing Association, and taught classes in home missionary work at the college. Shortly after accepting the position of treasurer of the General Conference in 1875 she was united in marriage with William Conqueror Sisley, an architect and builder, born in England. He had come to America when he was fourteen years of age. He was the architect and builder of the Battle Creek Sanitarium, Union College, Walla Walla College, Keene Academy, Dr. J.H. Kellogg's house and many other buildings in America, South America, and Australia.

Elder Uriah Smith officiated at their wedding. Their marriage was a very happy and devoted one lasting fifty-seven years. From 1896 to 1900 W. C. Sisley was manager of the Review and Herald Publishing house at Battle Creek. They worked hard together pioneering in educational, medical and publishing institutions. They moved to Nebraska, lived in a barn at first while they were helping to found and build Union College. From 1901 to 1918 they lived in London, England, building and planning schools, publishing houses and sanitariums.

Frederika was an excellent wife and mother while she was constantly active in secretarial work, teaching, and missionary endeavor. After many years of arduous labor Frederika and William retired to spend their last years next door to their daughter and her husband in Nashville. They had three daughters: Alice, Eulalia and Susie. William passed away on September 23, 1932, and Frederika would follow him in 1934.

10. Uriah Smith
September 19, 1876-September 20, 1877
(One year)

Age when elected Treasurer: 44 years old
Total Tithes when elected: $43,998.47
Per capita giving when elected: $4.38

See #1 of Secretaries for his bio.

11. Minerva Jane Loughborough Chapman
September 20, 1877-November 8, 1883
(Six years)

Age when elected Treasurer: 47 years old
Total Tithes when elected: $47,176.56
Per capita giving when elected: $4.03

Born: October 29, 1829, in Victor, New York
Died: April 25, 1923, in Battle Creek, Michigan. She was 93 years old.

John Loughborough had a sister who also left her mark on the pages of Adventist history. Minerva Jane Loughborough was born on October 29, 1829, in Victor, New York. She was the daughter of Nathan and Minerva Loughborough. She became an Adventist early in life and remained a firm and consistent follower even though her husband, Oscar A. Chapman, never became an Adventist.

On March 16, 1857, Minerva and Oscar were united in marriage. Sometime before the Civil War, Mr. and Mrs. Chapman went to LaSalle, Illinois, and later to Terre Haute, Indiana, while he worked in railroad services. When the Civil War began he worked in the navy doing duty on various warships. The Chapmans moved to Battle Creek in 1866. Very soon after arriving in Battle Creek Mrs. Chapman joined the Review and Herald staff which then numbered eleven persons, including Elder James White, the president of the institution.

Minerva's first work was as a typesetter. Her ability and faithful service soon led to her advancement to the position of secretary and then treasurer. She was then elected editor of the *Youth's Instructor* in 1875, a position she held until 1879 and again from 1884 to 1889. Concurrently, she served for six years as the treasurer of the General Conference, the third and last woman to hold this position.

The 1885, 1886 and 1887 *Yearbooks* list her as corresponding secretary of the General Conference. She remained with the Review and Herald Publishing Association twenty-six years retiring in 1893. She remained fifty-seven years in Battle Creek and was a member of the Battle Creek church where she was a tireless home missionary and a faithful member of the Sabbath School. She passed away in Battle Creek, Michigan, in 1923 at 93 years of age.

12. Archibald Robbins Henry
November 8, 1883-October 17, 1888
(Five years)

Age when elected Treasurer: 44 years old
Total Tithes when elected: $96,418.62
Per capita giving when elected: $5.53

Born: January 28, 1839, in Bonaparte, Iowa
Died: June 26, 1909, in Battle Creek, Michigan. He was 70 years old.

Archibald Henry was the son of Harvey and Cornelia Robbins Henry. He was born near Bonaparte, Iowa, seven years before Iowa was made a state and taught school until the Civil War. His father was a Methodist minister so he had very early religious training. In 1862 he was a student at Simpson College of Indianola, Iowa. When the Civil War started so many students enlisted that the college was suspended. Archibald was among those who answered his country's call for soldiers and enlisted in the Thirty-Fourth Iowa Infantry. He was promoted several times until he became a lieutenant. For some time he was the acting adjutant of the regiment serving in that position three years until the close of the war when he returned to Iowa and to teaching.

In 1865 he married Elizabeth Cottie. Henry was an extremely capable businessman and owned a bank in Iowa. Around 1877 he was converted to Adventism. At the encouragement of James and Ellen White he sold his bank in 1882 and moved to Battle Creek to replace Henry Webster Kellogg as financial manager of the Seventh-day Adventist Publishing Association. To accept this call meant to forsake his own business and forgo a liberal salary as a banker and learn a new and untried business at a greatly reduced salary. He left his business in Iowa and came to Battle Creek. He held this position until 1897.

From 1883 to 1888 he served as treasurer of the General Conference and oversaw the finances of many other Adventist institutions. He was a board member of nearly all early Adventist medical and educational institutions in the Western United States. He also visited Europe in the interests of denominational institutions. He also found time to operate his own lumber and building business in Battle Creek and was a shrewd businessman and a born leader of men.

Mrs. White reproved him several times for his secular and unspiritual business practices. In 1888 she spoke about his opposition to A. T. Jones and E. J. Waggoner's message on righteousness by faith. On March 10, 1897, Henry was dismissed from the Review and Herald and retired to his lumber business. He brought a lawsuit against the Seventh-day Adventist Publishing Association. Mrs. White reproved Henry and Harmon Lindsay by letters from Australia for their secular practices of finance.

In the end Henry repented, printed a long letter of repentance in the *Adventist Review*, dismissed the lawsuit, and remained in the church (unlike Harmon Lindsay who left the church and became a Christian Scientist).

13. Harmon Lindsay
October 17, 1888-February 17, 1893
(5 Years)

Age when elected Treasurer: 53 years old
Total Tithes when elected: $163,129.23
Per capita giving when elected: $6.20

See #8 for his bio.

14. William Herbert Edwards
February 17, 1893-February 19, 1897
(Four Years)

Age when elected Treasurer: 38 years old
Total Tithes when elected: $350,690.56
Per capita giving when elected: $9.37

Born: April 6, 1854, in Danvers, Massachusetts
Died: September 23, 1938, in Takoma Park, Maryland. He was 84 years old.

William Edwards was born and grew up in Danvers, Massachusetts, and later graduated from a prestigious business college in Boston. In 1877 he and his parents attended a series of meetings in Danvers and were baptized by D. M. Canright and C.W. Stone. The next year he was invited to connect with the Review and Herald Publishing Company in Battle Creek, Michigan, as manager of the wholesale and retail book department.

He continued at work until 1888 when he was appointed secretary and cashier of the Review and Herald. From 1891 to 1901 he served as General Conference treasurer, secretary-treasurer of the General Conference Association, and treasurer of the Foreign Mission Board. From 1901 to 1918 he was successively treasurer of the Michigan Conference, secretary-treasurer of the Lake Union Conference and secretary-treasurer of the Northern Union Conference.

After World War I he ran a print shop at the General Conference until his death in 1938. He gave nearly 52 years of continuous service to the Adventist cause. He married a college student, Mary A. Bierce, of Iowa in 1878, who was also employed at the Review and Herald. They had a daughter, Ethel.

15. Anderson Grant Adams
February 19, 1897-October 21, 1900
(Three years)

Age when elected Treasurer: 34 years old
Total Tithes when elected: $363,415.16
Per capita giving when elected: $6.43

Born: July 16, 1862, in Ohio
Died: December 14, 1936, in Seattle, Washington. He was 74 years old.

Anderson Adams was the son of Albert and Martha Mcdowell Adams and was born in the state of Ohio. His family moved to Wisconsin when he was three years old, and then to Minnesota where he grew up and became an Adventist.

He married Florence Coomer, a dressmaker, who died in 1957. They had two daughters, Ruth and Chloe. Besides being the treasurer of the General Conference he was the secretary and auditor of the North Pacific Union and editor of their paper, *The North Pacific Union Gleaner* from about 1906 to 1910.

Adams left the church for a number of years but renewed his commitment in his later life and stayed faithful until his death in 1936. One of the poems he wrote to affirm his renewed faith was published in the *West Michigan Herald*, on April 5, 1905.

Is It Worth While.

Is it worth while, dear brother.
Worth while for you and me.
To let the light of truth shine out
Across life's troubled sea!

Or, shall we stand here waiting;
While the breakers loudly roar.
And perishing souls about us
Go down ere they reach the shore?

Was It worth while for Jesus,
With love so great and free
To leave his home in heaven:
And die for you and me?

Oh yes, you answer quickly.
Worth while for the light to shine!
Worth while that we reflect that light.
Through our brief years of time.

—A. G. Adams, Battle Creek, Michigan

16. Harvey Melville Mitchell
April 19, 1901-March 27, 1903
(Two years)

Age when elected Treasurer: 53 years old
Total Tithes when elected: $578,628.13
Per capita giving when elected: $7.40

Born: March 26, 1848, in Morrow County, Ohio
Died: December 6, 1904, in Academia, Ohio. He was 56 years old.

Harvey Mitchell was a Methodist in his early life. It was not until he was thirty, in 1878, that he became an Adventist. Once he became an Adventist he was a very faithful, capable and willing worker.

Harvey's parents were Andrew and Martha Kilgore Mitchell and he was born and lived his life in Ohio, graduating from one of the best business colleges there. On August 13, 1875, Harvey married Hattie Flack and they had two children: Lorin Clyde and Daisy Lillian. Hattie's mother, Sarah Dickerson Flack, was the fourth child in a family of eight sisters and one brother.

The youngest sister, Phoebe Dickerson Harding, was the mother of Warren G. Harding, the 29th president of the United States. Phoebe's husband and son, Drs. George T. Harding, Senior and Junior, founded Harding Psychiatric Hospital in Columbus, Ohio. Harvey's older brother, Pastor David K. Mitchell, married Clara Dickerson, another sister of Phoebe Dickerson Harding.

The first record of H. M. Mitchell working for the church is in the *Adventist Yearbook* for 1889 when he was the Ohio state canvassing agent. By 1890 he was also one of the directors of the Mount Vernon Sanitarium and the vice-president of the Tract and Missionary Society. In his early ministry Elder Mitchell gave presentations on keeping financial books and business records to the Ohio Tract and Missionary Society. He was probably ordained in 1893 and the 1894 yearbook also shows him as a trustee of Mount Vernon Academy.

Elder Mitchell's first wife, Hattie, died in 1879 and he married Rebecca Brown on June 16, 1897. After serving two years as treasurer of the General Conference, he suffered from dropsy and died at his home during the time of the Young People's Convention when the Conference Committee and several other ministers were present to speak words of comfort to his family.

17. Irwin Henry Evans
March 27, 1903-May 13, 1909
(Six years)

Age when elected Treasurer: 40 years old
Total Tithes when elected: $684,030.54
Per capita giving when elected: $8.82

Born: April 10, 1862, at North Plains, Michigan
Died: November 24, 1945, in Takoma Park, Maryland. He was 83 years old.

Irwin Henry Evans was born in Michigan of Seventh-day Adventist parents. At age twelve he was converted and baptized and then attended Battle Creek College. It was his desire even as a child to be a minister and he used to go out and preach to the stumps on his father's farm. He entered the ministry at the age of twenty and did his internship in Kentucky. In 1886 he returned to Michigan as a pastor and in 1891 he became president of the Michigan Conference. He held this office for six years, and then was made a member of the General Conference Committee and president of the General Conference Association, the legal agency of the General Conference.

It was evident that he had executive and business ability and he was elected and appointed to the offices of president of the Mission Board, president and manager of the Review and Herald, and treasurer of the General Conference. In 1900 Evans was sent to Europe to settle the business problems of the Christiania Publishing House, which was facing bankruptcy.

In 1887 he married Emma Ferry who died in 1903. They had three children: Arthur Henry, Jesse Ruth, and Jerome Fargo. In 1904 he was united in marriage to Adelaide B. Cooper, then editor of the *Youth's Instructor*.

He and Adelaide went as missionaries to the Asiatic Division (1909-1913), and later he became president of the North American Division (1913-1918), and president of the Far Eastern Division (1919-1930).

Then he served as a general vice president of the General Conference until 1936, and a field secretary from 1936 until his retirement in 1941. From 1931 to 1941 he was also head of the Ministerial Association. He wrote several books, including *The Preacher and His Preaching, Ministry of Angels, The Way of Divine Love,* and *This Is the Way.*

Elder Evans was very interested in the development of the Adventist Theological Seminary and on several occasions taught homiletics there. He was a man of iron will but a gracious spirit. He was a friend and father of young ministerial students and encouraged and counseled them in their careers. He invested a considerable amount of energy in developing the *Church Hymnal* and wrote the hymn "Welcome, Day of Sweet Repose."

18. Walter Tingley Knox
May 13, 1909-May 11, 1922
(Thirteen years)

Age when elected Treasurer: 50 years old
Total Tithes when elected: $1,218,243.46
Per capita giving when elected: $12.07

Born: July 4, 1858, in Pittsburgh, Pennsylvania
Died: November 11, 1931, in Mountain View, California. He was 73 years old.

Walter Knox was an Independence Day baby, born on the 4th of July. His parents, Matthias and Eliza Knox, sent him to Canada to receive his grammar and secondary education at Grimsby College, a boarding school. He went to California at age sixteen seeking relief from malaria and he spent his young manhood in Southern California. At age twenty one he was converted and joined the Methodist Church. On December 8, 1885, he married Barbara Bell Childs and to this union a little girl, Barbara Maude, was born.

Through Bible study and personal research Walter accepted the doctrines of the Adventist Church in 1889. Almost immediately he entered denominational employment. He is listed in the yearbook as being ordained in 1894. From 1897 to 1900 he was president of the California Conference. At the 1901 General Conference session he was elected president of the newly organized Pacific Union Conference when it comprised all of California, Nevada, Utah, Alaska, Hawaii and Mexico. He held this position until 1904. In 1905 and 1906 he served as president again of the California Conference.

Elder Knox was a keen businessman and able administrator and in 1909 was elected to serve as treasurer of the General Conference. As treasurer he began working out the details of a financial program that would supply funds for the mission program of the rapidly expanding Church. In 1909 the General Conference voted that all Sabbath School offerings would go to missions and in 1912 the Thirteenth Sabbath overflow plan started, with India as the first recipient. The birthday offerings for new work started in 1919. These plans provided great impetus to the expansion of the mission program and outreach activities.

Knox moved to Mountain View, California, after his service as treasurer of the General Conference and while there he was chairman of the Board of Trustees of the Loma Linda Medical College and a member of the Pacific Press board of directors.

19. John Luis Shaw
May 11, 1922-May 26, 1936
(Fourteen years)

Age when elected Treasurer: 51 years old
Total Tithes when elected: $4,230,230.04
Per capita giving when elected: $20.26

Born: September 5, 1870, in Central City, Colorado
Died: July 22, 1952, in Loma Linda, California. He was 81 years old.

John was born into a Seventh-day Adventist family and was baptized at the age of fourteen. He entered Battle Creek College at sixteen and graduated from its scientific course in 1893. After graduation he was called to Union College as dean of men and teacher. Before beginning work at Union College he was married to Bessie L. Owens in 1893.

He later taught in Claremont Union College, South Africa. Returning to the States for the General Conference session in 1901, he was ordained to the gospel ministry by Elders Daniells, Prescott, and Spicer and asked to go to India. It was in India that their two children, Bessie and Horace, were born.

Elder Shaw was editor of the *Oriental Watchman* in Bombay, and in charge of the field of India from 1901 to 1912. He was unable to endure the heat during much of his twelve years in India and was in poor health most of the time. On his return to America he served as principal of the Washington Foreign Mission Seminary and from there came into the General Conference and educational work and later was one of the mission board secretaries.

From 1913 to 1915 he was secretary of the General Conference Department of Education and edited *Home and School Magazine;* then four times he served as one of the assistant General Conference secretaries. In 1922 he was elected treasurer of the General Conference and he served until 1936. He and Bessie moved to California to be near their children but his health continued to decline and Bessie died in 1939. During retirement he served for a time as chairman of the board of the Loma Linda Medical School. Eventually his health became so bad that from 1938 until the time of his death he was a patient at Loma Linda Sanitarium.

20. William Edward Nelson
May 26, 1936-July 10, 1950
(Fourteen years)

Age when elected Treasurer: 52 years old
Total Tithes when elected: $6,429,703.46
Per capita giving when elected: $26.50

Born: July 20, 1883, in the Dakota Territory
Died: May 10, 1953, in Takoma Park, Maryland. He was 69 years old.

The patriarch of the Nelson family, Elder Nels Peter Nelson, left his native land of Denmark in 1886 and came to Iowa. In 1867 he married Miss Andrea Kier. To this union were born seven sons and two daughters. In the spring of 1871 the patriarch moved in a covered wagon to Turner County, Dakota where he settled on a homestead, living in a sod shanty for six years. Someone shared with him the precious truths of the Third Angel's message in a printed brochure. Nels and Andrea studied carefully and accepted the message. N. P. Nelson later became a pastor and the president of the Dakota Conference, Nebraska Conference, and the Southwestern Union Conference.

When his son William Edward, the youngest of the boys, finished elementary school he was baptized by his father and William became a member of the Swan Lake church. In 1898 William moved with his parents to Lincoln, Nebraska, and a little later attended Union College.

In 1904 he received the Bachelor of Science degree from Union and enrolled the following year for graduate work at the University of Nebraska. While there he accepted the position as head of the Department of Science at Walla Walla College, where he remained until 1916, when he was elected president of Southwestern Junior College in Keene, Texas.

On June 18, 1907, William married Susan Shively, a graduate nurse from the Boulder Sanitarium. Together through many years they influenced thousands of youth by their counsel and example. William

Nelson proved to be an excellent administrator and moved from the classroom to school leadership. He had an innate ability to select a capable faculty, to persuade students to reach high standards, and to win the support of church and conference leaders.

From Texas he was called, in 1922, to the presidency of Pacific Union College, a position he held for thirteen years. In 1934 he was invited to become educational secretary for the General Conference. In 1936 he was elected treasurer of the General Conference, a position he held for fourteen years.

21. Chester Lozere Torrey
July 10, 1950-June 16, 1966
(Sixteen years)

Age when elected Treasurer: 55 years old
Total Tithes when elected: $27,728,250.32
Per capita giving when elected: $73.60

Born: May 19, 1895, in Marshalltown, Iowa.
Died: November 8, 1975, in Loma Linda, California. He was 80 years old.

Chester's childhood was plagued by the deaths of several of his family members. His brother Glenn died in 1902. His sister Rhea died in 1907 and another sister, Vera, died in 1908. The following year his father, John Vest Torrey, died in 1909 of cancer at age 48. His father had migrated to the state of Washington before he passed away and Chester grew up there.

His mother, Ella Waugh Torrey, soon remarried to George Kelly. His mother was the stabilizing factor in Chester's life. She was active in the work of the Women's Christian Temperance Union, in the Sabbath School, and in Harvest Ingathering. Chester began his work for the church as a colporteur and assistant evangelist and soon married Doris Abigail Stewart, on September 22, 1916, and they moved to Battle Creek, Michigan, for further studies. In 1918 and 1919 Chester served a short stint in the United States Army. Elder C.L. Torrey then served as treasurer in the New England Sanitarium and Hospital and then went to Poona, India in 1924 where he served as Secretary-Treasurer of the Southern Asia Division. Later he would serve as the Secretary-Treasurer of the Far Eastern Division and also the Inter-American Division before serving as the Treasurer of the General Conference from 1950 to 1966.

It is said that Elder Torrey had a tender heart for the needs of the people. He was a Christian gentleman at all times. The Torreys also experienced the loss of several of their children. They buried one daughter in Battle Creek, Michigan, and another daughter, Virginia Louise, in Poona, India. The son, Dr. Robert Torrey, was a graduate of Loma Linda Medical School. Elder C. L. Torrey passed away on November 8, 1975, in Loma Linda, California, at age 80.

22. Kenneth Harvey Emmerson
June 16, 1966-April 16, 1980
(Fourteen years)

Age when elected Treasurer: 48 years old
Total Tithes and offerings when elected: $92,295,960.39
Per capita giving when elected: $108.02

Born: April 4, 1918, in Forest Grove, Oregon
Died: February 4, 2004, in Hendersonville, North Carolina. He was 85 years old.

Ken was the child of Harvey and Hazel McLean Emmerson. The Harvey Emmerson home was at Pacific Union College where both their boys attended college. While attending PUC Ken Emmerson studied business and also met, fell in love with, and then married Dorothy Ayars, in 1938.

Dorothy Ayars was born of missionary parents, Ernest and Irene Ayars, in South America. They were deeply involved with founding the college in Peru. Dorothy's earliest memories were of this time in Peru. Later the Ayars also spent time helping to begin the college in Chile. Finally, before returning to the United States on permanent return, they served at the college in Argentina.

Soon after Ken and Dorothy graduated from PUC they accepted a call to the mission field and traveled to Cuba. Traveling in the wartime 1940s was understandably difficult. Kenneth Emmerson was serving in Cuba when he became one of the few missionaries on active duty to be drafted to serve in the US military. He went ashore on D-Day plus 2 and served in the Allied headquarters in Paris. He remembered signing the payroll checks for General Dwight Eisenhower.

After the war Ken resumed his service for the church, serving as Union Treasurer for the Mexican Union, associate treasurer for the Inter-American Division, and then treasurer for the South American Division.

In 1960 he was invited to serve as an associate treasurer of the General Conference. Then in 1966 he was elected to join President Robert Pierson as Treasurer of the General Conference. He served in that position until his retirement in 1980 in Walla Walla, Washington. Soon after retiring he was invited to be a GC field secretary, with assignments at Loma Linda University, Pacific Press, and Harris Pine Mills. Completing 45 years of denominational service, he retired again to Hendersonville, North Carolina, where he passed away in 2004 followed by his wife Dorothy in 2006.

The Emmerson's daughter, Anita, married Robert Folkenberg, who would become the president of the General Conference. The Emmersons had two sons, Robert J. and Richard K.

Former General Conference president Neal Wilson once said about Emmerson, "Sometimes people mistakenly assume that denominational financial officers are cold technicians, only interested in counting money. Ken was a competent business and spiritual executive. His greatest satisfaction was in helping to solve problems so as to fulfill the highest possible soulwinning expectations of God's people."

23. Lancelot Lewis Butler
April 16, 1980-June 27, 1985
(Five years)

Age when elected Treasurer: 61 years old
Total Tithes when elected: $398,880,407
Per capita giving when elected: $202.19

Born: November 17, 1918, in Adelaide, Australia
Died: August 18, 2004, in Sidney NSW, Australia. He was 85 years old.

The health work was responsible for bringing the Butler family into the Adventist Church. In 1889 Australian church leaders felt that the time had come to establish a representative sanitarium and hospital in Sydney, Australia. They finally settled on a twenty-nine hectare plot of land in Wahroonga, Australia.

It was far away from the center of the city and some called it the "Wahroonga Wilderness." Mrs. White, who was living in Australia at that time, made a special trip to inspect the site. She was driven in a horse and buggy to the site and when she saw the property, she exclaimed, "This is the place!"

Dr. Merritt G. Kellogg drew up a plan for a 100-bed, multi-storied hospital. Construction began but finances ran short. The medical director made a visit to a businessman who made a large donation to complete the building. The sanitarium was officially scheduled to open on January 1, 1903.

Before the official opening date, the sanitarium had accepted its first paying patient. Lewis Butler, a businessman and property owner in the Wahroonga district, fell seriously ill with rheumatic fever and was given forty-eight hours to live. In desperation the family transported him in a horse-drawn cab over the rough, stony ground to the still unfinished sanitarium. Dr. Kress and his nursing staff, through God's intervention, succeeded in saving his life.

Lewis Butler was deeply impressed with the ideals of the institution and the people who served there. During his convalescence, he read literature and after taking Bible studies, accepted the Adventist faith.

Over the years, four generations of Butlers have served the church. Lewis Butler's son, Alan Butler and his wife Hazel Hoskins, had a son named Lancelot Lewis Butler.

Lance, as he was called, would become a respected church businessman and treasurer. In 1946 Lance Butler married Peg Peacock. They had three sons: Robert, Donald and Rodney and one daughter, Sue. Butler would help steer the finances of the church during the erection of their new multi-rebuilding of the Sydney Adventist Hospital in 1971-1973. His highly valued service to the church included serving as treasurer of the former Australasian Division from 1968 to 1980 and finally as treasurer of the General Conference from 1980 to 1985.

Lance Butler implemented the construction of and move into the new General Conference office headquarters in Silver Spring, Maryland. He also prepared and drew up plans for the Pacific Adventist University in Port Moresby and initiated and oversaw the construction of the Adventist Alpine Village in New South Wales.

He died in Australia in 2004 at age 85.

24. Donald Floyd Gilbert
June 27, 1985-June 29, 1995
(Ten years)

Age when elected Treasurer: 54 years old
Total Tithes when elected: $456,783,830
Per capita giving when elected: $175.16

Born: October 8, 1930, near Black Hills, South Dakota
Retired in Arkansas, 84 years old (2015) and still counting.

Don Gilbert was born in South Dakota and lived his first eighteen years there, attending Plainview Academy. His parents, Floyd and Alice Gilbert, had two son, Don and his brother Orlo. Orlo taught music and directed the orchestra for many years at Southern Adventist University. His parents taught at Ozark Academy.

Don married Irene E. Julius in 1951 while he was attending Union College. He dropped out of school for a short while to earn money to continue his studies. Don planted a crop each summer in Lincoln, Nebraska, got his tractor and harvested the crop each year until he was able to finish school. Don graduated in 1955 as a business major and Irene graduated from Union College a year later in 1956. They have two children, Russell and Katherine, and each child has given the family two boys (four grandsons).

Don began his career as a teacher at Sandia View (1955-1960) Academy, then taught and was treasurer at Ozark Academy (1960-1961). From 1961 to 1974 he was treasurer of the South China Island Union Mission, living in Taiwan, and from 1977 to 1981 he was treasurer of the Far Eastern Division, living in Singapore. From 1981 to 1984 Don was the treasurer of the Iowa-Missouri Conference.

In 1984 he was invited to Takoma Park, Maryland, as assistant treasurer of the General Conference where his main assignment included international transportation of missionaries and other church workers and the processing of GC staff and departmental expenses. He was elected treasurer of the General Conference in 1985 and served for ten years.

After he retired he moved to Gentry, Arkansas, about a mile from Ozark Academy where he used to work and where his father had retired. His hobby is buying and fixing up old tractors. He belongs to an antique tractor club and has four old tractors. He also uses the tractors to plow his nineteen acre piece of farmland and to haul the wood he cuts to burn in his woodstove in the winter time. Don is a member of the board of Adventist Heritage and of Ozark Academy and a member of the finance committee of the local Adventist Church there.

25. Robert Lee Rawson
June 29, 1995-April 18, 2002
(Seven years)

Age when elected Treasurer: 58 years
Total Tithes when elected: $886,303,088
Per capita giving when elected: $172.14

Born: January 2, 1937, in Mt. Vernon, Ohio
Retired in Arizona. 78 years old (2015) and still counting.

Bob Rawson was born in Ohio into an Adventist family and attended Mount Vernon Academy. Both of his parents, Bruce and Irma Rawson, were nurses trained under Dr. Harry Miller, the China doctor. After attending Emmanuel Missionary College (Andrews University) for three years, Bob subsequently graduated from La Sierra University in 1960 with a Bachelor of Science in Business Administration.

Bob's first job after graduating from Andrews University was in the patients' business office at Loma Linda Hospital. Then he worked as a business manager/treasurer for Garden State and Mount Vernon Academies before going to the Philippines in 1968. Until 1976, he served in the Asia-Pacific region as business manager for Philippine Union College, and then as treasurer for the church's Far Eastern Division in Japan for three years before going to Singapore.

When he returned to the States he worked as treasurer in Iowa and Oregon. He was ordained in 1977 in Nevada, Iowa. Rawson also served as vice president for finance of the Adventist Media Center in Thousand Oaks, California, from 1977 to 1983. He was GC treasurer from 1995 to 2002. Ten years into his retirement, he was called to act as president of ADRA International while they searched for a new president.

Rawson married Carolyn Lounsberry from Illinois in 1958 and they had four sons: Richard, Robert (who passed away at age 29 from cancer), and twins, Timothy and Terry (married to sisters and live next door to each other). Although now retired, he keeps busy playing a little golf and serving on several boards, among them the Pacific Press Publishing Association and Gospel Outreach.

26. Robert Ernest Lemon
(April 18, 2002-July, 2015)
(Thirteen Years)

Age when elected Treasurer: 53 years
Total Tithes when elected: $1,161,698,944
Per capita giving when elected: $152.66

Born: March 14, 1949, in Kongolo, Zaire
Retired at the 2015 General Conference in San Antonio

Robert E. Lemon, elected as Treasurer of the General Conference in 2002, has served in various treasury functions over the years. Born in Kongolo, Zaire, to missionary parents Philip and Elizabeth Lemon, mission has always been his passion. Bob speaks both English and Swahili. He attended Gem State Academy and received his B. S. degree (Business Administration) from Columbia Union College in 1972. While attending college his studies were interrupted while he served for a time in the military in the White Coats at Fort Detrick.

Lemon began his work for the church in 1972 as an accountant for the Hackettstown Community Hospital in Hackettstown, New Jersey. He returned to the place of his birth in 1974, serving as an auditor for the Zaire Union and then treasurer of the union located in Lubumbashi, Zaire. He was ordained to the gospel ministry on September 1, 1979, at the Triangle Church, Lubumbashi, Zaire.

In 1982 he relocated to the Africa-Indian Ocean Division (now the West-Central Africa Division), in Abidjan, Cote d'Ivoire, as an assistant treasurer.

Following mission service in Africa, Lemon returned to the North American Division in 1985 where he served as chief accountant at Andrews University, and where he also earned a master's degree in Business Administration (MBA, 1988). He then served as treasurer of the Alberta Conference and then the Seventh-day Adventist Church in Canada. In 1995 he joined the treasury office of the Adventist world church as associate treasurer and undertreasurer before his election as General Conference Treasurer in 2002.

Lemon was married to Sherry Wiebold on June 7, 1970, by his father, Elder Philip F. Lemon. Sherry is a graduate of Walla Walla College (1966). The couple has two grown children, Tami Thombs and Jamie (James Wayne), and three energetic grandsons (Austin, Parker, and Jackson).

27. Juan Rafael Prestol-Puesán
(July 3, 2015- -)

Age when elected Treasurer: 68 years old
Total Tithes when elected: $2,314,826,002
Per capita giving in 2012: $190.69

Born: June 19, 1947, Island of Hispaniola, in Colonial City, Santo Domingo, Dominican Republic
Prestol is the current Treasurer and Chief Financial Officer of the Adventist Church.

Juan Rafael Prestol-Puesán's early life placed him in an environment conducive to learning and faith development. A fourth generation Seventh-day Adventist, he was baptized at age 14.

Although both Juan and Belkis Dominiguez were citizens of the Dominican Republic, they never met until they went to Puerto Rico to attend the Antillian Adventist University in Mayaguez. After graduation Juan married Belkis in 1969 and their home soon had two daughters, Johanna and Idaía. They returned to the Dominican Republic where Juan worked as the assistant treasurer and accountant for the Dominican Conference and Belkis worked as an elementary school teacher. Rapid growth of the church in the island made it necessary to divide the Dominican Conference into two conferences, and Prestol was appointed secretary-treasurer of the new North Dominican Mission. When Prestol arrived at his new appointment he had to find property, set up a new office, and completely furnish it from scratch. Soon it was necessary to divide again, and there were soon four conferences on the Dominican side of the island.

In 1977 the Prestols moved to Berrien Springs, Michigan, where he attended Andrews University. While there he obtained a Master's degree in Business Administration. After graduation Juan began work in the Treasury Department of the Greater New York Conference. While there his wife attended college in Westbury, Long Island, and received a degree in accounting in 1984.

In 1987 the Prestols were invited to the Atlantic Union Conference, where Juan served as treasurer and trust services director and Belkis served as accountant. In early 1993 they received an invitation to work in Moscow in the nearly organized Euro-Asia Division which served a population of 300 million people and comprised the five unions that existed in the former USSR. He would serve there with Ted and Nancy Wilson who also accepted a call to be the president of that new division.

Arrangements were made for the Wilsons, Prestols and two other families to study Russian in a large room at the General Conference headquarters for six to seven hours a day for about four months. So today, Juan Prestol who is bilingual in English/Spanish also has a working knowledge of Russian and Portuguese.

After three years in that large division Juan was called to be the associate treasurer of the North American Division and two years later the treasurer. In 2007, Elder Prestol was asked to become the Undertreasurer of the General Conference, a position he held until he was elected the chief financial officer of the world church in 2015 in San Antonio.

Today the Prestol family includes a son-in-law, Samuel L. Janniere, and two grandchildren, Elisa Amelie and Ian Samuel. Juan was ordained in 1976 to the gospel ministry.

On Friday, September 12, 2014, Juan Prestol successfully defended his dissertation, which was titled "An Exploratory, Correlational, Self-Rater Study on Authentic Leadership Values of Adventist Local Conference Chief Financial Officers in the United States." Juan used the Authentic Leadership Questionnaire administered by MindGarden as his instrument to gather data from CFOs (treasurers) and their colleagues in 50 denominational fields in the U.S. The results revealed that in addition to financial expertise, a global organization must also pay close attention to the leadership values and practices of its CFOs. He was officially awarded his Doctor of Philosophy degree from the School of Education, Andrews University, in 2015. At his acceptance of the position Prestol-Puesan said that the Church has to be concerned about change. "The volatility of the world's financial markets has made managing the church's funds more challenging. Changes in interest rates in some parts of the world can mean a profit or loss of millions of dollars. Changes in financial markets, changes in world economies, perhaps a few surprises—we still have to trust in the Lord. But we also have to be careful and mindful managers of the Lord's funds. Another challenge is changing demographics."

Picture Credits
(for those not identified in captions)

List of Abbreviations

ANN	Adventist News Network, Silver Spring, Maryland
CAR	Center for Adventist Research, Andrews University, Berrien Springs, Michigan
EGWE	Ellen G. White Estate, Silver Spring, Maryland
GCA	Archives of the General Conference of Seventh-day Adventists, Silver Spring, Maryland
LLU	Loma Linda University Library Digital Photo Archives
OUA	Oakwood University Archives, Huntsville, Alabama
Review	Adventist Review or Adventist Review and Sabbath Herald, Silver Spring, Maryland
WWC	Walla Walla University Archives
T	Top
B	Bottom
L	Left
R	Right

p.17: T: GCA; B: Adventist Heritage Magazine, July, 1974, p.10. **p.18:** TR: LLU; B: Library of Congress Reference Numbers LC-US2-16225 and LC-US262-119343. **p.19:** T: CAR; B: The Atlantic Union Gleaner, March 5, 1987, p.5. **p.20:** T: CAR. P.21: CAR. **p.22:** all three pictures from Dr. Cyrus Oster. **p.23:** Krystal Eskildsen, Review, February 27, 2015. **p.24:** T: Review, February 24, 2011, L.W. Onsager and J. R. Nix, B:Yvonne Kroehler. **pp.28, 29:** all pictures from GCA. **pp. 35-43**, all pictures from EGWE except **p.39:** B: Kreigh Collins, artist, North American Informant, March-August, 1965, p. 12. **p.40:** B: www. victorissa.com/collection/this is the very place, May27, 2014. **p.42B and 43T:** www.Revelation1412.org. Nader Mansour, Feast Days and the Present Truth, pp, 3, 4. **p.47:** T: EGWE, B: Harry Anderson, Review, 1944. **p.49:** TL/R: LLU, B: EGWE. **p.50:** T: stock/standard photo from webpage; B: EGWE. **p.51:** T: EGWE, B: Don May. **p.52:** T: LLU; B: EGWE. **p.55:** EGWE; **p.56:** TL: GCA, TR: Review, August 8, 1918. **p.57:** all 3 pictures, OUA. **p.59:** BL: CAR. **p.64:** Sons of the North, Lewis Harrison Christian, p.61. **p.65:** T: LR: CAR, B: L: EGWE R: CAR. **p.66:** all from EGWE. **p.67:** EGWE. **p.68:** T: EGWE, B: CAR. **p.69:** T: LLU, B: Lake Union Herald, August 5, 1969, p.11. **p.70:** all from CAR. **p.71:** TB: CAR. **p.72:** T: EGWE, B: OUA. **p.75:** Guide, Thomas Dunbebin, artist, May 3, 1967. **p.76:** GCA. **p.77:** T: OUA, BL: CAR. **p.78:** WWC. **p.79:** T: Alfred Vaucher, Francophone Adventist Archives, B: OUA. **p.80:** T: OUA. **p.83:** TL: EGWE, TR and B: CAR. **p.84:** TL and TR: EGWE, B: LLU. **p.85:** TR: GCA, TL: CAR, BL: EGWE, BR: US Passport Office. **p.86:** TR: 1918 Yearbook, B: LLU. **p.87:** TL: EGWE, TR: GCA, B: Review, May 2, 1918, p11. **p.88:** T: GCA, B: Washington Adventist University Weiss Library. **p.92:** TL: GCA, TR: CAR, B: Milton College Preservation Society. **p.93:** TL and BL/R: CAR, TR: LLU. **p.94:** T: LLU, B: CAR. **p.95:** T: CAR, B: Review October 4, 1984, p.14. **p.96:** TL: LLU, TR: CAR, B: www.michiganwomens hall of fame.org. **p.97:** TB: Southern Asia Division. p.98: T: WWC, B: OUA. **p.99:** T: EGW, B: Review online, January 28, 2015. **p.104:** T: GCA, B: R. G. Pretyman, Australian Record, 9/9/68, p.7. **p.105:** T: Review, B: CAR. **p.106:** T: British Historical Archives, B: Cannibals and Headhunters of the South Seas, Charles H. Watson. **p.107:** Historic Images: Acme News Pictures, San

Francisco Bureau. **p.110:** T: GCA, B: GCA. **p.111:** TB: CAR. **p.112:** all pictures, CAR. **p.113:** T: Review, July 16, 1950, p.93, B: GCA. **p.114:** T: CAR, B: Review, GC Bulletin 5, July 17, 1 950, p.135. **p.115:** T: www.findagrave.com, B: OUA. **p.116:** OUA. **p.120:** L: LLU, R: EGWE. **p.121:** T: LLU, B: LLU School of Religion. **p.122:** T: LLU Health, B: www.findagrave.com. **p.123:** T: WWC, B: CAR. **p.124:** T: CAR, BL: GCA, BR: Review, June 23, 1950, p.247. **p.125:** T: Review, July 16, 1950, p.94, B: Eastern Tidings, December 1, 1936, p.2. **p.126:** T: LLU, B: OUA. **p.129:** L: CAR, R: www.findagrave.com. **p.130:** TB: www.findagrave.com. **p.131**: T: YouTube, April 1, 2013, LetsPrayTV, B: NPUC Gleaner, August 3, 1987, p.5. **p.132:** T: Canadian Union Messenger, September 6, 1967, p.20, B: www.findagrave.com. **p.133:** TB: WWC. **p.134:** TL: North American Informant, March-August, 1965, p. 15, TR: Review, 1966, June 24, p.5. B: Review, July 25, 1962, p.5. **p.135:** T: Review, June 30, 1966, p.11, B: CAR. **p.139:** Review. **p.140:** T: GCA, BL: Review, July 13, 1975, p.1, BR: Review, November 2, 1978, p.5. **p.141:** TB: CAR. **p. 142:** T: CAR, B: Review. **pp.143-145:** DeWitt S. Williams photos. **p.146:** TL: Ministry, June, 1975, p.40, TR/BL: ibid. p.37, BR: Review, May 1, 1980, p.30. **p.147:** TL: Ministry, June 1975, p.39, TR: CAR, B: Review, October 26, 1978, p.1. **p.152:** T: GCA, B: Clarice Wilson. **p.153:** T: Clarice Wilson, TR/BL: GCA, BR: College yearbook. **p.154:** T: Review, November 12, 1925, p.4, B: GCA. **p.155:** T: Pacific Press Publishing Assn. B: Review. **p.156:** T: Clarice Wilson, B: Review, January 20, 2011, p.10. **p.157:** B: Andrews University. **p.158:** T: Columbia Union Visitor, August 1, 1985, p.3. **p.159:** TB: Review, January 20, 2011, p.9, 11. **p.160**: T: Review, November 28, 1991, p.7, B: Clarice Wilson. **p.161:** T: WWC, B: Southern Tidings, November 16, 1978, p.12. **p.162:** T: Ebony, November, 1979, B: DeWitt S. Williams. **p.168:** T: GCA, B: Review, July 9, 1990, p.9. **p.169-175:** Robert Folkenberg, **p.175:** B: Gerry Chudleigh. **p.176-180:** Robert Folkenberg. **p.185:** T: GCA, BL: Review, May 1999, p.13; BR: Review. **p.186:** T: British Historical Archives, B: Review. **p.187:** T: Review, B: ANN. **p.188:** TB: ANN. **p.189:** T: ANN, B: Rajmund Dabrowski, ANN. **p.190:** TB: ANN, Tor Tjeransen. **p.191:** T: ANN, B: Jan Paulsen. **p.192:** T: ANN. **p.193:** T: Josef Kissinger, B: Andrews University. **p.194:** Joel D. Springer, Review, July 2, 2000, p.10. **p.199:** Review, January 20, 2011, p.9. **p.200:** T: GCA, BRL: Clarice Wilson. **p.201:** TB: Clarice Wilson. **p.202:** T: Ted Wilson, B: Gina Wahlen. **p.203:** T: Adventist Review Online, October 11, 2014, B: ANN, Southern Asia Division. **p.204:** T: Ansel Oliver. **p.205:** Ansel Oliver, B: Thailand Mission. **p.206:** SUD, B: Southern Asia Division. **p.207:** T: SukHee Han, B: Vietnam SDA Mission. **p.208:** TB: Ansel Oliver. **p.209:** T: Vietnam SDA Mission, B: Review. **p.210:** Review. **p.212-245**: all from GCA except **p.240:** Sue Franz Smith. p. **248-290:** GCA.

Back cover: CAR

General Conference leadership at the 1913 General Conference Session held in Takoma Park, Maryland. The General Conference Committee, including elected officers, presidents of union conferences, heads of departments, and superintendents of mission fields. The row in front, beginning at the left: R. C. Porter, president of the Asiatic Mission Field; I. H. Evans, president of the North American Conference; L. R. Conradi, president of the European Conference; W. T. Knox, treasurer of the General Conference; A. G. Daniells, president of the General Conference; J. N. Loughborough; G. I. Butler; S. N. Haskell; O. A. Olsen. Second row: H. R. Salisbury; W. A. Ruble, Medical Department; W. A. Spicer, General Conference secretary; Mrs. Flora Plummer, Sabbath-school Department; N. Z. Town, Publishing Department; M. E. Kern, Missionary Volunteer Department; J. L. Shaw; C. B. Stephenson. Third row: Frederick Griggs; W. B. White; Charles Thompson; S. E. Wight; E. E. Andross; B. G. Wilkinson; M. N. Campbell; E. T. Russell. Above third row, beginning at left: C. H. Jones; J. W. Westphal; F. W. Spies; W. W. Prescott; W. C. White; Dr. H. W. Miller, Medical Department; H. S. Shaw; G. F. Watson, W. C. Sisley; O. E. Reinke; Allen

Moon; G. B. Thompson, secretary North American Conference; L. P. Tieche; W. J. Fitzgerald; J. E. Fulton; H. F. Schuberth; J. T. Boettcher; J. G. Oblander; C. W. Flaiz; J. F. Huenergardt; U. Bender; J. C. Raft; L. H. Christian; E. R. Palmer. The picture was printed in the *Signs of the Times*, July 8, 1913, p.10.

CPSIA information can be obtained
at www.ICGtesting.com
Printed in the USA
FSOW04n1650050417
32749FS